# Little Hinges

## Lee Merrick

WESTBOW®
PRESS
A DIVISION OF THOMAS NELSON
& ZONDERVAN

WestBow Press books may be ordered through booksellers or by contacting:

WestBow Press
A Division of Thomas Nelson & Zondervan
1663 Liberty Drive
Bloomington, IN 47403
www.westbowpress.com
1 (866) 928-1240

ISBN: 978-1-4908-5155-6 (sc)
ISBN: 978-1-4908-5156-3 (hc)
ISBN: 978-1-4908-5154-9 (e)

Library of Congress Control Number: 2014916162

Printed in the United States of America.

WestBow Press rev. date: 5/20/2015

# Contents

# Introduction
## They Had Forgotten God's Words

When the Babylonians defeated the Israelites in 586 BC, they completely destroyed Jerusalem and exiled the survivors to Babylonia. Fifty years later, some of the religious Jews had been allowed to return to Jerusalem to rebuild their cherished temple.

Twenty years after returning, their new temple was finished. The Israelites expected God to bless them for their restorative work, but He did not. Instead, they faced years of drought, famine, poverty, and oppression by the non-Jews who had moved into the area surrounding Jerusalem.

Gradually, these faithful Jews became hard-hearted and indifferent to their rules of worship and their offerings to God. They questioned His love and loyalty for them and continued to drift farther away from His commands. Their skepticism led to a moral and spiritual anemia, which fostered permissiveness and independence. The men started divorcing their wives, marrying the foreign women nearby, and adopting many of their pagan customs. They neglected God's rules and started to depend on their own resources for their survival. They grew proud of their achievements, which bolstered self-confidence and eventual arrogance.

God was disappointed in His remnant of once-devoted Jews, so He sent His last true prophet, named Malachi, to them sometime between 425 and 400 BC to rekindle their faith by assuring them He still loved them. It didn't work. God's words through Malachi couldn't explain His lack of blessings. The people had forgotten God's love. They still respected Him, so they continued to observe Jewish holidays. They still feared His wrath, so they tried to placate Him by performing Jewish rituals. But their hearts no longer burned with desire to please their one, almighty God.

When Malachi started preaching God's words to the Israelites, they made arrogant attempts to floss over their blatant sins by asking questions like: "How have we shown contempt for your name?" (Malachi 1:6e); "How have we defiled you?" (Malachi 1:7); "How are we to return to you?" (Malachi 3:7c); "How do we rob you?" (Malachi 3:8b); and, "What have we said against you?" (Malachi 3:13).

Malachi realized by their questions that this generation of Israelites no longer knew God's laws. They no longer knew right from wrong, so he could go no further with them. He had come to a stand-off with the Israelites. They were disappointed with God, and God was disappointed with them. Malachi knew he wasn't getting God's love through to them. Their worship of God was false, but the truth would have to come later.

God saw the problem. Fear of the LORD through the Mosaic Law and the ancient prophets of the Old Testament, was not working. His people were stepping around Him and making up their own rules. Upset with their rebelliousness and foolish apostasy, God left a disasterous judgement against the disobedient priests and people for their multiple sins.

Using Malachi as His bewildered spokesman, God told them they would be destroyed by fire on the Day of the LORD (Malachi 4:1). He also left a blessing for any obedient Jews in the future, who would revere His Name and repent for their sins. He promised them that the "sun of righteousness"—the Messiah—would rise and heal them physically and spiritually (Malachi 4:2).

After Malachi finished his prophecy, the voice of God was silent for four hundred years. The next prophet on the scene was John the Baptist, who boldly preached, "Repent, for the kingdom of heaven is near" (Matthew 3:2). John was right. The kingdom was definitely near, because the King was actually in their midst.

Jesus had not been revealed yet, because the God-fearing Jews of the first century AD didn't know God's original laws either. Their religious rules had progressively changed over the centuries, and the people had no idea they were committing any sins!

In the next three years, it was Jesus who taught the Israelites what was wrong in their lives and what they could do to make their lives better under Roman occupation. It was Jesus who introduced a new covenant, and showed mankind how much God really loves the world.

After Jesus' death, burial, resurrection, and ascension, it was His apostles who never forgot the extent of His love. It was His apostles who shared the kingdom of God with the rest of the world. They were the facilitators, or little hinges, who opened a large door to a much better world for all of us.

Part of the kingdom is here on earth right now. So if you are eager to know God's peace, empowerment, and meaning for your life, you are heading in the right direction!

Most of the kingdom will come when Jesus returns as King of kings to avenge His continual opponents. So if you are yearning for world peace, for all injustices to be dealt with immediately, and for all things to be made right again, this book is for you!

# 1
## Religious and Political Oppression

When Jesus was born, many Jews had stopped believing in their old Scriptures. They had lost faith in the promises that had been made seven hundred years earlier about a virgin who would give birth to a Son who would be called Immanuel, meaning "God with us" (Isaiah 7:14), and about the Messiah, who would be born in Bethlehem, the town of King David (Micah 5:2). They were tired of waiting for the Savior, who would lead them to everlasting peace. They had lost interest in learning anything more about their patriarchs, judges, kings, or prophets. They knew their rich history and their mistakes, but their knowledge wasn't very consoling. They were sick of being ruled and oppressed by foreign powers.

Revolutionists among the people were quite influential. They were convinced there would be no peace until they fought for it. They believed Israel would be saved only through uprisings, blood, and death. They talked about a king who would come one day and free Israel by armed forces … a military genius who would shellac Herod, deliver them from foreign governments, and make them masters of the whole world!

Faithful Jews like Joseph, Mary, Elizabeth, Zachary, and John the Baptist disagreed with the revolutionists and resisted their influence. They realized their ancestors had been destroyed, because they had lost faith in God's power and had started to depend on their own might. These few, faithful Israelites didn't want to repeat the shortcomings of their ancestors. They were determined to rely on God's promises and fully believed peace would only come from Him. They were willing to wait for their Deliverer to come. They also knew He would come for everyone, not just the Jews. He would be the Master of the world and bring peace to every believer. What they didn't know, though, was that He was going to come twice, first as a humble servant and second as the King of kings!

Sadly, all the doubtfuls and hopefuls were led astray by their religious leaders—and by their rich and powerful Jewish citizens,

1

who collaborated with the Romans and fattened their fortunes by betraying and oppressing the rest of their fellow Jews.

Annas, the high priest of Herod's temple when Jesus was born, was a prime example of good faith gone bad. He was a Sadducee, who didn't believe in resurrection or a future life. (He was sad, you see!) He lived for himself and all the gusto he could get in the here and now.

Herod the Great had been appointed as the king of Palestine by the Roman Senate in 40 BC. His principal duties were to collect taxes for Rome and to keep the peace in a little part of Palestine called Israel, especially in its main provinces of Judea and Galilee. These two provinces were hotspots in the Roman Empire. The Israelites were known as being very difficult people to rule.

Herod was an Arab from Ashkelon, in southeast Palestine, and the Israelites hated him. His ancestors had been forced to convert to Judaism, but the Jews never accepted him as anything more than a cruel and merciless representative of a foreign power. He was an Arab puppet who taxed them unfairly for the benefit of Rome.

Herod tried to placate the Israelites by extravagantly rebuilding their beloved temple in Jerusalem, but it didn't work. They knew he paid for it, but because it was designed by Jewish architects and built by Jewish labor, they barred Herod from entering any part of it when it was finished.

The Jewish temple had always been a symbol of the continuity of the Jewish race. It gave them their sense of belonging in the world and in their community. They could gather to their peculiar selves without being intruded upon or contaminated by the pagan world, with its multiple, fickle gods. The Israelites sacrificed animals there for God's forgiveness of their sins, and under the very noses of their foreign rulers, they prayed daily to be delivered from their conquerors and oppressors.

The worshippers were not allowed to bring their own sacrifices to their temple. They had to buy the lambs and doves from the priests, who set up stalls in the outer courts and then charged their own people five times what the animals were worth. Even more fraudulent, the people had to buy them with Jewish coins, which were available in the temple by special concession but forbidden anywhere else. Since Israel was a prisoner state in the Roman Empire, it was occupied by legions of the Imperial Army. Only silver empire coins bearing the head and sign of Caesar could be used to buy or sell anything. In order to buy sacrifices in their temple, the worshippers had to exchange their empire coins for their former Jewish coins in yet another unfair transaction. The money changers exploited them also, by giving them maybe half of what the empire coins were worth.

Guess who reaped the profits from the money changers and the merchants in the temple? Annas, the high priest in charge of the temple. He owned the concessions and controlled all the priests. He also controlled the banks. Annas was the political boss of Jerusalem and a crooked one. He bargained secretly with King Herod and then told the Jewish people what they had to do.

Herod liked Annas, because he kept the money rolling in and kept the Jews in line. Annas liked Herod, because he let him keep his wealth and his honorable position of high priest. They understood each other perfectly and worked well together to keep Caesar happy. Taxes and tranquility, taxes and tranquility ... taxes, taxes, taxes, and tranquility.

Annas and his crooked cronies kept the money rolling in for Rome and also for themselves. They nearly doubled the amount of taxes on the heavily overtaxed citizens and then hired tax collectors (publicans) to collect them. It was a devious system which enabled them to bank the unjust half in their own accounts and hide their dirty work.

Annas sold himself out completely to Herod and Rome. He became the leader of the forty wealthiest families in Israel by cheating his fellow Jews. He knew his head would be the first to roll if Herod were ever overthrown, so to protect them both, Annas organized a secret police to ferret out rebellions and punish any revolutionary leaders. *Pax Romana* was a forced peace—and a very effective one.

The oppressive religious and political wheels were rolling pretty smoothly until Jesus was born in Bethlehem. Four things happened quickly to vex Annas and Herod and to renew ancient faith in prophecies: (1) the announcement about the birth of their Savior that blessed night by the angel of the Lord to the shepherds, (2 and 3) the testimonies of His divine nature, which were given a week later in the temple by both Simeon and Anna, and (4) the wise men who arrived months later by following a supernaturally bright star to worship the newborn king.

The people began wondering if their old prophecies were true after all. King Herod began to worry they were and wasn't about to tolerate a competitive king in his domain, even if he were only an infant.

# 2
## Renewed Faith

Humble shepherds were the first people who came to visit the newborn Jesus. They were tending their sheep that night, minding their own business, when they were suddenly engulfed in a bright light and became terrified! They clearly heard the voice of an angel, who said, "Do not be afraid. I bring you good news of great joy that will be for all the people. Today in the town of David, a Savior has been born to you; He is Christ the Lord. This will be a sign to you: you will find a baby wrapped in clothes and lying in a manger" (Luke 2:10–17).

Right after this announcement, the heavens opened, and a host of angels filled the night sky. They were praising God and singing to all the ages: "Glory to God in the highest, and on earth ... peace to men on whom His favor rests" (Luke 2:14). Today we sing, "Peace on earth to men of good will." This is *not* a peace for everyone. It's an inner peace for those who learn His will, for His favor will always rest on those who continually try to walk in His ways.

When the angels left, the shepherds hurried off and finally found Mary, Joseph, and baby Jesus, who was, in fact, lying in a manger! After seeing them with their own eyes, the shepherds spread their incredible story in Bethlehem and then returned to their flocks. They praised God for His message to them and for His gift to the entire world. Isaiah's seven-hundred-year-old prophecy had been fulfilled: "For to us a child is born, and to us a son is given" (Isaiah 9:6).

The spiritual revelation continued eight days later, when Joseph and Mary obediently took Jesus six miles to the temple in Jerusalem for His presentation to God, and for the rites of purification for Mary. Every woman who gave birth in those days was required to offer a sacrifice of a lamb or two doves for bringing another sinner into the world. A priest had to make atonement for her before she would be "clean" again in God's eyes (Leviticus 12:8). As dictated by Jewish law, "Every firstborn male is to be consecrated to the Lord" (Exodus 13:2). Jesus was to be set aside, or made holy, for service to the Lord.

At the temple, they met an old man with extraordinary faith named Simeon. He lived in Jerusalem, but fully believed the angel's report about the birth of the Messiah in Bethlehem. God had promised Simeon that he would see Christ the Savior before he died, and the Holy Spirit had moved him to go to the temple at the same hour Mary and Joseph arrived with their infant. (Luke 2: 27)

When Simeon saw baby Jesus, he took Him in his arms and praised God. He knew Jesus was the Savior the world had been waiting for, for nearly a thousand years. He turned to Mary and announced God's plans in public: "This child is destined to cause the falling and rising of many in Israel … the thoughts of many hearts will be revealed … and a sword will pierce your own soul, too" (Luke 2:34, 35). In other words, (1) Jesus would influence many people to support Him, and they would live forever with Him. The ones who rejected Him would die. (2) Some initial supporters would walk away from Him. (3) Mary would be hurt by the controversies that would eventually surround Him.

Right after Simeon's statements, an old prophetess named Anna came up to them. She was a teacher of the Old Testament and a true spokeswoman for God. She had been widowed after only seven years of marriage and lived out the rest of her life as a resident in temple quarters. She served as an attendant there and worshipped God day and night.

Anna was about eighty-four years old when she recognized baby Jesus as the Messiah. She, too, gave thanks to God. She announced that Jesus would be the one to release Jerusalem from all its sins and pay the price for them Himself (Luke 2:36–38).

King Herod heard the stories of the shepherds' bizarre night and the fervent testimonies in the temple. He worried about the implications. Messiah? Savior? Deliverer? He certainly hoped not! He liked his job. He protected it. He even killed family members who threatened to take it. He was the king of Palestine. Therefore, *he* was the king of the Jews, who lived in a small part of it. He didn't want anyone to "deliver" the Jews from under his authority. Nor did he want anyone disrupting the policed peace in Israel. He was well aware of the turbulence and anguish simmering in the hearts of the oppressed Jews. It wouldn't take much to ignite it into mass hysteria and a major revolt. He didn't want Roman soldiers pouring in to crush a revolt. Any order of that kind from their peacefully minded emperor Caesar Augustus would cost him his job, and very possibly, his head!

Months later, Herod the Great heard that wise men from different areas in the East were now in Jerusalem to worship the newborn King of the Jews. Herod was greatly disturbed. He summoned the Jewish religious leaders to learn about their ancient prophecies. He asked where their Messiah had been predicted to be born.

The religious leaders quoted the prophet Micah and told Herod that Christ would be born in Bethlehem, a village just south of Jerusalem: "But you, Bethlehem, in the land of Judah, are by no means least among the rulers of Judah; for out of you will come a ruler who will be the shepherd of my people Israel" (Micah 5:2).

Herod then sent for the magi and tried to learn when their star first appeared. That would tell him the approximate age of his newest competition. He sent the magi to Bethlehem and asked them to report back to him so that he could worship the newborn also (Matthew 2:8).

The wise men found Jesus in Bethlehem. He was no longer in the stable; he was in a house (Matthew 2:11). They presented Him with gifts of gold, frankincense, and myrrh. That night, all of them had the same dream. They were warned not to return to Herod, so they returned to their countries by different routes and were never heard from again (Matthew 2:11, 12).

The story of the magi underscores the fact that God sent Jesus to earth to save all people, Jews and non-Jews. There were people from other populated regions in the world who were also waiting for the Jewish Messiah to be born. The magi did not make their long journey to merely acknowledge the birth of the newborn King. They came to *worship* that newborn king! They knew He would be called Immanuel, meaning "God with us," and they knew He would be their King one day.

After the wise men left Bethlehem, an angel of the Lord appeared to Joseph in a dream. The angel told him to take his family to Egypt,

7

because Herod was searching for Jesus to kill Him (Matthew 2:13). The family left for Egypt and stayed there until Herod died a few weeks later. Then they returned to Nazareth, their hometown in the province of Galilee.

The four Gospels combined (Matthew, Mark, Luke, and John) give us the most information we have about Jesus before He began His mission, but they tell us very little about His childhood. God didn't think it was relatively important, so we have to roll with the intentional gap. We don't need to know if Jesus ate all His vegetables. We do need to know who He was and what He came to do. God sent Jesus for a reason, which is carefully explained in the Bible. His readiness and mission are paramount. Trivial facts about His youth are not. In Scripture, His infancy ended with the statement, "And the child grew and became strong; he was filled with wisdom, and the grace of God was upon him" (Luke 2:40). The next thing we learn about Jesus is what happened to Him in Jerusalem, when He traveled there as the twelve-year-old who was "filled with wisdom."

Jesus had been invited to go to Jerusalem with others from His community for the Passover feast. It was common in the first century to travel in large groups for safety, so Jesus tagged along with His extended family and friends. When it was time to return to Nazareth after the one-night ceremonies, Jesus was mistakenly left behind.

Mary and Joseph returned to Jerusalem the next day and searched the city for Jesus. They finally found him in the temple, where, much to their surprise, Jesus was actively engaged in advanced theological discussions with the religious leaders! The scholars, onlookers, and parents were all amazed with His grasp of Scripture. It was way beyond anyone's expectations of a twelve-year-old.

Quoting Scripture was one thing. Understanding and applying it to principles was something entirely different! Most Jewish boys could quote Scripture. They had to complete extensive studies before they were accepted into their religious communities as responsible, law-abiding men at the age of thirteen. A six-year-old could recite the entire Torah (Genesis, Exodus, Leviticus, Numbers, and Deuteronomy). A twelve-year-old could recite the entire Old

Testament. Most of them knew the words of God, but they didn't know God. Their knowledge was academic but not applicable. They knew Scripture but didn't understand it, so they couldn't apply it to their lives.

Jesus was different. He understood Scripture. His questions were excellent. His responses were profound, because He knew God and was filled with divine wisdom. He understood the will of God and was starting to apply it to His daily life. He wanted everyone, including self-absorbed religious leaders, to know the real God. He wanted them to understand what God actually wrote and why He wrote it.

When Jesus' parents arrived and approached Him, Mary asked, "Son, why have you treated us like this? Your father and I have been anxiously searching for you" (Luke 2:48). They had been separated for two days, but Jesus didn't seem to be worried or concerned about their anxieties.

Surprised by her question, Jesus asked, "Why were you looking for me? Didn't you know that I had to be in my Father's house?" (Luke 2:49). Jesus was not being rude. He was honestly amazed that His parents had been desperately searching for Him. Jesus knew He had done the right thing under the circumstances. He had gone to a safe, public place for the night, under the watchful eyes of trusted adults in the temple. He thought He had made it easy for His parents to find Him.

Jesus knew His identity. He knew He had a unique relationship with His heavenly Father and a unique mission to accomplish for Him. He assumed His earthly parents knew that also, but they didn't, because they had not understood His reply about His Father's house (Luke 2:50). Jesus' parents, as well as His future disciples, would always have problems understanding His numerous revelations. It would take time for them to grasp who He really was and what He had come to do. Their gradual enlightenment, though, would not be up to Him. Their understanding would come from God the Father.

Jesus returned to Nazareth with His parents and continued to obey them (Luke 2:51). His relationship with His heavenly Father did not nullify His duty to honor His parents. He simply submitted His divine abilities to the will of God (John 4:34), and continued to mature. "And Jesus grew in wisdom and stature, and in favor with God and men" (Luke 2:52).

During the next approximate eighteen years, Jesus worked hard to become fully human in every way—intellectually, physically, spiritually, and socially. He learned all about human needs, human miseries, and fallen human nature. Then, when He was about thirty years old, God called Him to begin His mission (Luke 3:23).

# 3
## Beginning of Public Ministry

Jesus left Nazareth to be baptized by John the Baptist, His second cousin. Their mothers were first cousins. Their grandmothers were sisters.

John's parents were considerably older than Mary and Joseph. When they died, John moved to the desert wilderness. There he wore clothing made of camel's hair, with a leather belt around his waist, and he ate locusts and wild honey (Mark 1:6).

God had called John to fully immerse people in water as a testimony of their repentance and submission to His will. (John was the first person who ever *baptized* anybody!) God told John to watch for a man on whom His Spirit would descend and remain, for that would be the man who would eventually baptize believers with the Holy Spirit (John 1:33).

Jesus found John immersing people in the Jordan River near Jericho, just north of where the river flowed into the Dead Sea. He sauntered through the crowd of John's followers and down to the water's edge to the baptized, also. But John objected to Jesus' request (Matthew 3:14), because his baptisms symbolized repentance from sins, and he knew Jesus had never committed any sins.

Jesus told John He needed to be baptized so that He could "fulfill all righteousness" (Matthew 3:15). He wanted to identify symbolically with sinful humanity, because one day in the near future, His righteousness was going to cleanse and purify all people who believed in Him (2 Corinthians 5:21).

John complied and immersed Jesus in the Jordan River. When Jesus came out of the water, the Holy Spirit came down upon Him in the form of a dove. A voice from heaven came, saying, "You are my Son, whom I love; with you, I am well pleased" (Luke 3:22). John instantly knew the true identity of Jesus. He was the more powerful one coming after him, who would baptize with the Holy Spirit and fire. His cousin was the Son of God!

John also knew his own godly purpose in life. He was the forerunning voice, calling to "prepare the way for the Lord" (Isaiah 40:3). God chose him to announce that the time was right for the people to get ready for the arrival of their future King. "I am the voice of one calling in the desert: 'Make straight the way for the Lord'" (John 1:23).

The preparation was a spiritual one. God wanted His people to change their minds, hearts, and direction. He wanted them to learn what was wrong in their lives and turn from it. He wanted them to relearn His unchanged will for their lives and walk in His ways. He would gladly help them straighten their paths if they asked for His assistance. But He would never force His ways on them. As a champion of free will, He would always leave their choice of direction up to them. He loved them all more than they could possibly comprehend and hoped they chose well.

Immediately after being baptized, Jesus became empowered by the Holy Spirit. He was led out into the wilderness desert to confront Satan. There, Jesus took the first step toward destroying his evil kingdom (1 John 3:8b). He stayed there and fasted for forty days. He was attended by angels (Mark 1:13) and counseled by the Holy Spirit. He was tested by Satan to demonstrate He was the Son of God and to prove He could not be broken down or forced to fall away from God's will.

Satan's first temptation was physical. Satan knew Jesus was fasting and hungry. Knowing that humans need food for survival, he said, "If you are the Son of God, tell these stones to become bread" (Matthew 4:3).

Jesus answered from Scripture: "It is written: 'Man does not live on bread alone, but on every word that comes from the mouth of God'" (Deuteronomy 8:3). Jesus knew that bread might save a temporary, physical life, but only God's ways can ensure an everlasting life.

Satan's second temptation was spiritual. It dealt with supernatural beings. He took Jesus to the highest point of the temple in Jerusalem and dared Him to throw Himself down (Matthew 4:6). Then, he purposefully misquoted Scripture and said that if He was the the Son of God, He would be saved by the angels of God.

Again Jesus answered from Scripture: "It is also written: 'Do not put the Lord, your God, to the test'" (Deuteronomy 6:16). Satan knew better. He was trying to get Jesus to win the favor of the people by a spectacle instead of His messages or His righteousness. It didn't work.

Satan's third temptation was psychological. Knowing that most men want power, he told Jesus he would give Him all the kingdoms of the world, with all their splendor, if He would bow down and worship him (Matthew 4:8, 9). Jesus retorted, "Away from me, Satan! For it is written: 'Worship the LORD your God, and serve Him only'" (Deuteronomy 6:13). Satan did leave temporarily (Luke 4:13), but he continued to harass Jesus throughout the remainder of His short life.

Does Satan have the kingdoms of the world to give Jesus? Yes, absolutely! He rules the fallen world. He's the reason behind today's worldwide confusion, division, hatred, and violence. Satan knows that good will overcome evil when Jesus returns in glory as King of kings. But that doesn't deter him from trying to cause as much destruction as possible, or from trying to take more souls to fall with him.

# 4
## Hometown Bound

After successfully resisting Satan's temptation, Jesus left the Judean wilderness and headed north, toward the province of Galilee. He was walking back to His hometown in Nazareth, where He planned to announce His mission.

As He walked past John the Baptist, Jesus noticed that he was talking with two of his young disciples, Andrew and John, who worked together in a fishing guild. They lived in the small town of Bethsaida, near the Sea of Galilee, and they rented their boats out of nearby Capernaum.

Andrew and John worked very hard, but what little they earned went directly to pay their heavy Roman taxes. They couldn't even afford to eat the fish they caught in their own nets! Poor and hungry, they left their boats temporarily and headed south to the Jordan River, because someone told them John the Baptist knew the secret for living a happy life under Roman rule. They found John and were standing with him when Jesus walked by. John the Baptist announced, "Look, the Lamb of God" (John 1:36). Wondering if Jesus might be John's "secret," they started following Jesus.

Jesus turned back to them and welcomed their company. He invited Andrew and John to spend the day with Him and tell Him about all their problems. He didn't have to ask twice!

Jesus knew they were working hard but living miserable lives. He knew all about their frustrations, insecurities, and bleak outlooks. Nevertheless, He listened patiently and answered all their questions with a kindness that bound their hearts to His.

Neither Andrew nor John had ever heard anyone speak like Jesus. He used simple words and immense feelings as He talked about a new, invisible world of thoughtfulness and giving instead of selfishness and taking. He told them about His plan to tour small towns in the Palestinian provinces of Judea, Samaria, Galilee, Perea, and Idumea. He wanted to teach the disheartened villagers about this new world and assure them there really was a purpose in life. Their

14

lives mattered to God the Father, so they mattered to Him! He wanted to make them worth living.

Andrew wanted to hear more about this purpose in life, but he wanted his brother, Simon, to hear about it also. He left John with Jesus and raced back to Bethsaida to fetch Simon.

Simon was very skeptical of Andrew's "messenger-of-God-who-could-answer-every-question-in-the-whole-wide-world," but he left his nets to follow Andrew back to meet his newest mentor.

Jesus enthusiastically embraced Andrew's brother and said, "You are Simon, son of Jonah. You will be called Cephas" (John 1:42). The term *Cephas* means "rock" in Aramaic and is translated "Peter" in Greek.

As Jesus continued to enlighten His three young followers, Simon Peter grew equally impressed with everything he heard. His brother Andrew had truly found a caring, religious adviser, who wanted to teach the poorest people about the richest possibilities of life. Here was a man who was capable of bringing a warm light to anyone who was bewildered or frightened.

The four of them continued traveling north together for a few more days. Along the way, another friend of Andrew's joined them. His name was Philip, and he was also from Bethsaida.

It didn't take Philip long to realize that Jesus was offering them a new hope for a better world in this life and the next. He, too, wanted to hear more about this new world, but he left them briefly to find and enlist his good friend Nathanael (also known as Bartholomew). When he found him, he breathlessly described whom he had met and excitedly encouraged Nathanael to join their group. "We have found the one Moses wrote about in the law, and about whom the prophets also wrote—Jesus of Nazareth" (John 1:45).

Nathanael walked with Philip to meet his extraordinary teacher. When they arrived, Jesus said, "Here is a true Israelite in whom there is nothing false" (John 1:47). Perplexed by his introduction, Nathanael asked Jesus how He knew anything about him. Jesus told him He had seen him sitting under a fig tree before Philip called him (John 1:48). Nathanael immediately acknowledged His supernatural clairvoyance and proclaimed, "Rabbi, you are the Son of God, you are the King of Israel" (John 1:49). Jesus humbly replied, "You believe because I told you I saw you under the fig tree. You shall see things greater than that" (John 1:50).

Jesus didn't affirm Nathanael's declaration. Nor did He disclose anything more about Himself that day. He would reveal His true identity and full mission little by little. It would take three years, and He would control every event leading up to and including His death on the cross.

A few days later, they were all invited to a wedding in Cana, another small town in Galilee. The bride's parents were friends of Jesus' mother. This is where Jesus performed His first public miracle. He felt sorry for the family hosting the celebration. They had little money and ran out of wine for their guests early in the evening. Jesus turned six large, stone jars of water into very good wine. The guests were never aware of the calamity, but the servants certainly were, and so were Andrew, Peter, John, Philip, and Nathanael. Jesus "revealed His glory, and His disciples put their faith in Him" (John 2:11). Word about Jesus of Nazareth quickly spread throughout the region, and His public ministry began.

Jesus saw the eager enthusiasm of His five disciples. He knew they were awed and excited, but He didn't call them to follow him permanently for almost another year. He wanted them to learn much more about Him and about His mission before they committed themselves fully to Him by leaving their homes, their families, and their former lives. Until then, He only expected them to find Him when they could leave their work for a few days, and listen carefully to more of His messages about a new life worth living.

After the wedding, Jesus visited Capernaum with his mother, brothers, and young disciples. Capernaum was located on the northwestern shore of the Sea of Galilee, about two and one-half miles west of where the Jordan River emptied into it. It was on a major trade route from Damascus to the seaports in Egypt, so it was busy, exciting, wealthy—and *very* corrupt. Jesus saw it as an economic center and a perfect stage from which to send His messages around the world. He decided to settle there after going to Jerusalem for the celebration of Passover.

When Jesus arrived at the magnificent temple in Jerusalem, He was frustrated by the blatant exploitation there by the money changers and the merchants who were selling lambs, bulls, and doves. He made a whip out of some cords and drove all the profit-makers out of the courtyard with it! He overturned the tables of the money changers and declared, "How dare you turn my Father's house into a market!" (John 2:16). His actions and accusations made breaking news once again! More and more people began to follow Him to hear or see what He might say or do next. He was a one-man show not to miss.

# 5
## Nicodemus

One night that same week in Jerusalem, a fine man named Nicodemus left secretly to speak with Jesus. He went at night because he was a leader of the Jewish people, and his reputation was at stake. He was a Pharisee, so he was committed to certain beliefs, including their additional set of oral traditions. He was also a member of the ruling council (the Sanhedrin) that had once sent a committee to investigate John the Baptist when he started to attract crowds of Jewish worshippers, before Jesus began His ministry.

Nicodemus learned from these committee reports that John started out by preaching: "Repent, for the kingdom of heaven is near" (Matthew 3:3), John denied being the Messiah, but he revealed that the Messiah was definitely present and actually walking among them (John 1:26, 27). Nicodemus wondered if Jesus of Nazareth could possibly be their Messiah, so he went to find out who Jesus really was. He also wanted to know more about the kingdom of heaven.

Jesus welcomed Nicodemus and informed him that he could not enter the kingdom of God unless he was "born again" (John 3:3). Jesus was referring to a new birth in which God imparts a spiritual life into believers. (The Greek word translated into "again" can also mean "anew" or "from above.") Nicodemus couldn't perceive such a spiritual rebirth. He thought Jesus was referring to some sort of second physical birth, so he asked Him how that might happen.

Jesus explained further that there are actually two realms in existence at the same time: a physical one of the flesh (the realm of humankind) and a spiritual one of the Holy Spirit (the realm of God). Flesh cannot make itself into spirit, so people cannot save themselves. They must be regenerated by God in order to live with Him eternally. In other words, they must experience a spiritual rebirth. They must be "Born of water and the spirit" (John 3:5). They must be born again. Only God can make flesh into spirit.

Enlightened by these new revelations, Nicodemus shifted into a higher, required gear and asked Jesus how people can be

18

spiritually regenerated. Jesus did answer his question, but first He rebuked Nicodemus for being a teacher of Hebrew Scripture and not remembering the prophets often used the word "water" as a reference to the Spirit of God. The phrase "born of water and the Spirit" came directly out of the scrolls of Isaiah: "For I will pour water on the thirsty land, and streams on the dry ground; I will pour out my Spirit on your offspring, and my blessing on your descendants" (Isaiah 44:3). Nicodemus should also have known about "new hearts" and "new spirits" from the scrolls of Ezekiel: "I will give you a new heart and put a new Spirit in you; I will remove your heart of stone and give you a heart of flesh. And I will put my Spirit in you to move you to follow my decrees, and be careful to keep my laws" (Ezekiel 36:26, 27).

After revisiting those necessary preliminaries with Nicodemus, Jesus then answered his question. He informed him that spiritual rebirth can only happen through the Son, the cross, and faith in both (John 3:13–15). His explanation led right into one of the most well-known verses in the Bible: "For God so loved the world, that He gave His one and only Son, that whoever believes in Him shall not perish, but have everlasting life" (John 3:16).

Jesus gave Nicodemus a panoramic glimpse of God's plan for salvation, but it was enough for him to realize the enormity of His assertions. Jesus was claiming to be the one and only Son of God ... the water poured out on the thirsty land ... the anointed One sent to save the world. Scripture doesn't tell us if Nicodemus ever connected all the dots and, thereby, accepted Jesus' messages and miracles as proof of who He claimed to be. Scripture does tell us most religious leaders did not accept His testimony (John 3:11, 32), so the public controversies continued and escalated.

# 6
## The Samaritans

After meeting with Nicodemus, Jesus spent time alone in the Judean countryside with some of His loyal disciples. He gave them His authority to perform baptisms. The disciples of John the Baptist didn't like the new kids on their block. They grew jealous of Jesus' increasing popularity and confronted John with their dismay. John knew it was time for him to step back. He explained to his disciples that people were right to flock to Jesus, because He had truly come from heaven. John encouraged his disciples to follow Jesus, also.

Jesus was aware that John's disciples, as well as the Pharisees, were beginning to focus on His influence. He didn't want to be drawn into any controversies over baptism this early in His public ministry, so He left Jerusalem and returned to Galilee with His followers. He returned through Samaria.

There were several roads going north from the province of Judea through the province of Samaria into the province of Galilee. Most Jews from Judea and Galilee avoided the Samaritans completely by traveling on the road near the Mediterranean coast, or the road on the other side of the Jordan River in the province of Perea. Jesus undoubtedly surprised everyone by taking the central road through the heart of Samaria, but there was someone there He needed to see.

The Jews didn't like the Samaritans. The pious Jews looked down their noses at their neighbors. The rift between them began centuries earlier, when the Northern Kingdom of Israel was defeated by the Assyrians in 722 BC. To prevent the Israelites from regrouping and revolting against the victors, the Assyrians exiled most of the Jewish leaders into areas of today's Iraq and replaced those families with non-Jews from surrounding countries who worshipped multiple gods. The remaining Israelites who survived the Assyrian invasion and not exiled, gradually started to marry the imported foreigners and adopt their pagan ways of life. The Israelites never stopped worshipping their one, almighty God, but they worshipped Him in addition to the lesser gods.

This was a mistake. A huge mistake. They stopped living to please God and started living to please themselves. Worse yet, they had no intentions of heeding any of the prophets' gloomy warnings, so they discarded most of their religious scrolls. The only books of Scripture they considered to be authoritative were those written by Moses: Genesis, Exodus, Leviticus, Numbers, and Deuteronomy. In doing so, they lost their identity and racial purity. Consequently, the God-fearing Jews of Judea and Galilee wanted nothing to do with the "partial" Jews of Samaria, whose beliefs had become so limited and diluted.

Jesus felt differently. He knew the Samaritans had once been godly Jews, who were misguided by secular kings and then overwhelmed by the foreigners who replaced their leaders and customs. He wanted to help them. His earthly mission was "to seek and save what was lost" (Luke 19:10). He considered the wayward Samaritans to be His lost sheep. He would find them, reveal His true identity, and teach them the truth about God's intentions. Then He would leave them with their free wills to choose their own destinies.

Jesus started His search in the central town of Sychar. He sent His disciples for food and then looked for a very specific social outcast … a woman of ill repute. He found her at a well, "Jacob's well." (The heart of Samaria was once the land of Abraham's grandson, Jacob, one of the cherished Jewish patriarchs.) When the woman came to draw water, Jesus asked her to give Him a drink. She was surprised, because she recognized Him as a Jew and knew He was forbidden to talk to a Samaritan, much less ask one for anything. He kindly informed her, "If you knew the gift of God, and who it is that asks you for a drink, you would have asked Him, and he would have given you living water" (John 4:10). He also told her that everyone who drinks her well water will get thirsty again, "but whoever drinks the water I give him will never thirst … it will become in him a spring of water welling up to eternal life" (John 4:14).

The perplexed woman missed His spiritual message completely. She wanted His "living water" so that she wouldn't have to draw her own water every day. It was hot, hard work.

Seeing her confusion, Jesus told her to go get her husband and return to Him. She answered honestly that she had no husband. Jesus knew that and replied, "You are right ... you have had five husbands, and the man you now have is not your husband" (John 4:18). Jesus focused on her sins and her spiritual need for a Savior. The woman focused on His supernatural knowledge of her morally dubious life and came to the conclusion that He was a divinely inspired prophet. She didn't know what Jesus was talking about, but she did know God was going to send them a divine prophet, who would teach them all things (Deuteronomy 18:15). She said, "I know that the Messiah is coming. When he comes, he will explain everything to us" (John 4:25).

With her prophetic lead-in statement, Jesus declared, "I who speak to you am he" (John 4:26). Jesus had found the woman He was looking for and made the first revelation of His true identity. The woman had found the Water of Life, which she had not known she needed.

Euphorically, she abandoned her water jar and hurried back to the townspeople. She cried out, "Come see a man who told me everything I ever did! Could this be the Christ?" (John 4:29). The woman's news, and her candor about her own depraved life, convinced the Samaritans to find Jesus and speak with Him themselves. They did and were so impressed with His words that they urged Him to stay longer, and teach them more. They were genuinely interested in everything He had to say.

Jesus stayed with them for two more days. He knew the Samaritans had been handicapped by their ancestors, who had tossed away so many major, religious scrolls. Because of that, they didn't know the real God. They were missing too many of His essential principles. They couldn't worship Him reverently (in human spirit and truth), because they couldn't comprehend an invisible God who was really part of their everyday lives. They worshipped Him once a week, but their worship was an external one, which merely conformed to religious rituals and celebrations.

Jesus stayed long enough to teach them the complete truth about God the Father through their missing Scriptures. He taught them that God wanted to regain His primary position in their daily lives and loved them enough to send His only Son to them. By revealing who He was, and what He had come to do, Jesus revived their beliefs in their Messiah and boosted their spirits. They knew He was the renewing fountain of water, spewing into everlasting life. He softened and enlarged their hearts. They would now be able to worship properly "in spirit and in truth" (John 4:23, 24).

We know the Samaritans accepted Jesus' revelations wholeheartedly, because they reported back to the woman from the well and said, "We no longer believe just because of what you've said; now we have heard for ourselves, and we know that this man really is the Savior of the world" (John 4:42).

The scorned woman had led the Samaritans to their salvation. They had a renewed hope for life and a purposeful reason to live. They would continue to live in harmony with God the Father, and they would support the chosen disciples one day in their near-future declarations of Jesus as King of kings and Son of God.

Success! Unopposed success for Jesus. The hearts of the Samaritans were open to Him. They had accepted Him as the Water of Life, and He had written every one of their names in the Book of Life. Win-win!

# 7
## The Nobleman

Another unlikely revelation and conversion occurred in Cana, after Jesus left Samaria and returned to the province of Galilee. The Galileans were excited to have Him back in their midst. They had heard about His first public miracle there and had seen Him in action in Jerusalem during the weeklong Passover festival, when He drove the money changers out of the temple with His whip. He was their new hero, and they hoped to see more dazzling performances!

There was another man in Cana who had walked twenty miles from his home in Capernaum to find Jesus. He was a nobleman, a royal officer in the service of King Herod Antipas. (Antipas was the son of Herod the Great and was called a king. But technically, he was the Tetrarch of Galilee from 4 BC to AD 39. He was only one of the four Palestinian rulers.)

The nobleman was a desperate man. His son was dying, so he walked all day to find Jesus. He had little appreciation of who Jesus was but knew He was his only hope. His son needed a miracle to live, so the nobleman needed to find the man who had changed water into wine.

When he found Him, he begged Jesus to walk back with him to heal his son. "Sir, come down before my child dies" (John 4:49). Jesus told him that his son would not die, and he could go back to him. The nobleman believed Jesus' promise and left for Capernaum. Along the way, his servants met him with the good news that his son's fever had left him at the seventh hour (John 4:52). When the nobleman realized his son's recovery corresponded precisely with the time he had spoken to Jesus, he knew Jesus was someone far greater than a mortal, miracle worker! He had spoken a word that produced results twenty miles away. He was a master of distance.

The faith of the nobleman soared. He believed Jesus twice. First, he believed in His promise, "Your son will live" (John 4:50). What was it about Jesus that calmed his worst fears and made him trust the miracle worker? His compassionate eyes? His gentle demeanor? His look of authority? He didn't know. There were no words to describe such a gripping awareness. Second, he believed in the Person. His wonderful presence, His encompassing aura, His thorough goodness, His special love for others, His awesome power. The nobleman's open heart to Jesus was contagious. He believed, and so did his entire household (John 4:53).

The nobleman had gone to Jesus in desperation and returned to his son with assured confidence. He knew little about Jesus of Nazareth, but he was anxious to learn His messages, understand His actions, and share them all with others. Jesus had given life back to his son and forth to him. He knew he had gained a new life with a solid foundation. It was a full, exciting life, and one definitely worth living.

# 8
## The First Rejection at Nazareth

The woman at the well led the Samaritans to their faith in Jesus, and the nobleman led his entire household (including the servants) to Him. Once Jesus revealed who He was and what He came to do, *all* of them accepted Him as the Son of God without second thoughts, reservations, or opposition.

The Judeans and Galileans, however, would be more difficult for Jesus to convince, because they had so many misconceptions about their coming Messiah. Most of the Israelites were waiting for a Jewish king to come rule the world. They expected a warrior Savior, with a supernatural genius for war and government, to lead them in a successful revolution against the Roman Empire, free them from all foreign rulers, and make them masters of the whole world forever. They expected a trinity of a patriot, a general, and a king. Jesus would slowly, ever so carefully introduce them to the trinity of God the Father, God the Son, and God the Holy Spirit.

Jesus began this introduction in his hometown of Nazareth, where He announced His mission as God's servant, spokesman, and prophet. He walked to the synagogue there on the Sabbath and respectfully stood to read the Word of the LORD from the scroll of Isaiah. He quoted, "The Spirit of the Lord is upon me because He has anointed me to preach good news to the poor. He has sent me to proclaim freedom for the prisoners, and recovery of sight for the blind, to release the oppressed, and to proclaim the year of the Lord's favor" (Luke 4:18, 19). With that announcement, He rolled up the scroll, handed it back to an attendant, and humbly sat down again as customary to teach the Word of God. He looked directly at the Nazarenes and said, "Today this Scripture is fulfilled in your hearing" (Luke 4:21).

The people were amazed over such a gracious presentation coming from a local boy without a rabbinic ordination. They didn't have any objections to His messages until He told them two stories about former prophets who had performed compassionate miracles

26

for non-Jews. When Jesus insinuated that His proclamation and restorations would also be extended to people of all races and religious backgrounds, His fellow Jews went berserk. They expected "the year of the Lord's favor" to favor them and only them. They knew that they were God's chosen people, and they weren't about to share His blessings with non-Jews. Enraged over Jesus' diversification plans, they marched Him out of town and actually attempted to kill Him by throwing Him off a cliff.

Undaunted by their belligerence, Jesus calmly walked right through the crowd and continued on His way (Luke 4:30). His supernatural escape didn't seem to faze them or smooth their ruffled feathers.

Their impulsive reaction didn't surprise Jesus, either. He had come to establish an entirely new kind of kingdom, one different from what anyone expected. He came prepared for opposition. He left Nazareth to let things simmer down. Jesus planned to return the following year, when His hometowners might understand His messages a little better.

# 9
## Jesus versus the Pharisees

When Jesus had heard that John the Baptist had been arrested for rebuking King Herod Antipas over his incestuous marriage to his niece, He knew John's ministry had come to an end, and His formal ministry needed to begin. He left Nazareth, moved his headquarters to Capernaum, and began to preach right where John left off, saying, "Repent, for the kingdom of heaven is near" (Matthew 3:2; Matthew 4:17).

Throughout the Gospels, Jesus preached about the kingdom of God over one hundred times! It was His main message and the summary of everything He taught. It was a beginning and an end. It was not a threat. It was an invitation into the kingdom of God right here on earth, as well as an invitation to life everlasting with Him after death.

The Greek word for repent is *metanoia,* which means to "change your mind." Jesus wanted people to change their way of thinking, because God was now in their midst and could empower them with everything they needed to survive the storms in their lives—if they would just draw closer to Him. He knew their lives could be much better and more fulfilling if they turned to and relied on Him.

His kingdom sermon was very popular. The people loved hearing Him say, "Come to me, all you who are weary and burdened, and I will give you rest ... for I am gentle and humble in heart ... my yoke is easy, and my burden is light" (Matthew 11:28–30). When He extended this invitation, He often had difficulty escaping from the crowds. The people wanted to capture Him and force Him to be king.

Repentance also refers to the desire to restore or build a good relationship with God. It starts by turning away from what is wrong and toward what is right. The problem was that the people no longer knew wrong from right, because some of their religious leaders had been subtly but progressively changing their basic Jewish laws for hundreds of years. Consequently, the law-abiding citizens had grown confused and overwhelmed.

The Israelites had never considered themselves to be lawmakers or law changers. They merely tried to understand the laws and honor God by obeying them. But the laws kept changing, and the taxes kept rising. They had no lives. They felt like slaves being driven by King Herod for the benefit of Rome, not for the benefit of their beloved Israel. Their slavery in addition to such treason, was doubly oppressing. Even worse, the majority of them were being exploited by their own flesh and blood.

Jesus felt sorry for them. To stop such oppression, He intended to expose the ulterior motives of their religious leaders, especially those of the Pharisees. How? (1) By revealing the hypocrisy of their leaders who preached God's commandments but turned a blind eye toward poverty, sorrow, illness, and handicaps; and (2) by challenging the authority of their religious leaders and getting them to show their hands … their cold, legalistic approach to Judaism.

Jesus knew He wasn't going to receive any awards from the political or religious gurus of His day for turning a light on bad situations. On the contrary, He knew He was about to incur their murderous wrath. His exposure of injustices was going to put Him in direct opposition of the rich, the powerful, and the orthodox teachers, who all used "religion" for their own selfish purposes. He was fully aware of the dire consequences He would face. The leaders would eventually kill Him to prevent further truths from being revealed to the commoners.

Jesus was prepared to die; it was part of His mission. He knew His opponents would kill His body, but they would never be able to kill His words. His messages would continue to spread through His chosen disciples, who would eventually fulfill Isaiah's prophecy by becoming the Light of the World (Isaiah 49:6). Ultimately, the followers of His disciples would continue to extend the kingdom of God until He returned as King of kings.

It was just about time to start asking His most loyal followers to stay with Him permanently, instead of traveling back and forth between their trades and His sermons, as they had been doing for the last year or so. He wanted them with Him every day and night now, so He could teach them His undoctored interpretation of Scripture. He knew that the pure laws God had handed down through Moses and the prophets were not necessarily the same ones being read to them in the synagogues of His day. His disciples needed to learn the difference between true doctrines and false ones. They also needed to understand His convictions, because He was going to publicly reproach their religious leaders, especially the Pharisees.

The Pharisees? Why in the world would Jesus oppose them? Weren't they good citizens? Yes, they were exemplary citizens and religious scholars, who were dedicated to teaching God's laws. But they were the ones who changed the laws the most drastically. They were the ones most directly responsible for making the lives of people so complicated and difficult. Did they change them overnight? No, they changed them very gradually, first to help the Jewish people be accepted by the Greeks and the Romans, and later, to help them gain more approval in God's eyes.

When the Greek and Roman Empires ruled Palestine (Israel and its surrounding provinces), the Jewish people yearned to be included in the new, upwardly mobile societies. To their dismay, though, they were ostracized as pious ancients firmly entrenched in their peculiar customs and beliefs.

That was true. The Israelites believed in one God, and they were surrounded by pagans who worshipped multiple gods. They had learned terrible lessons about worshipping wooden idols in addition to their one God Almighty, so they weren't going there again. But they wondered if they had to be so completely shackled by their religious parameters. Was there any way they could become part of the new worldly happenings without disappointing God? The Pharisees were the ones who said yes and stepped up to the plate to accommodate both the Israelites' desires and their own.

The Pharisees were a large religious sect of Jewish leaders who emerged in about 160 BC. They became religious role models for the God-fearing Israelites, because they were apparently descendants of the ultra-pious Hasidim. Because they controlled the synagogues, the Pharisees controlled a major portion of the Jewish population. They were always closely associated with the rabbis, because the rabbis were the ones who taught the religious laws in the synagogues. The Pharisees were highly educated and masters of Scripture, so the rabbis readily accepted their reasons for what should be taught. That's how the Pharisees began to relax God's original laws and change the laws by passing down their opinions and philosophies to the Jewish people through the rabbis.

The Pharisees thought they could relax the stringent laws just enough to open the hearts of an enlightening pagan society to their fellow Jews and still keep God happy. They were wrong. God watched the Pharisees lead His people away from Him by making them worldly instead of holy. The people and the Pharisees began concentrating on themselves, not on Him, and He was anything but happy.

There were two other major religious parties operating in the same era as the Pharisees. They were known as the Sadducees and the Essenes. Divine misconceptions were multiplying rampantly, because all three groups believed in the written laws handed down to the people through Moses, but beyond that, their beliefs were wildly different.

The Pharisees were the only ones who believed that God revealed some things to Moses that were written down (God's original written laws) and other things that were not written down (the oral laws, or traditions). To the Pharisees, both sets of laws were equally binding. Not to God, though, and not to Jesus, either. The oral laws were what caused the direct opposition between Jesus and the Pharisees.

The oral laws were originally developed by the ancient rabbis after the temple in Jerusalem was first destroyed by the Babylonians in 586 BC and the leading Jewish families were exiled. The Pharisees increased them in the first century BC and began honing them severely. By the time Jesus was born, the oral traditions of the Pharisees had become ridiculously trivial and incredibly burdensome.

Over the centuries, the written laws were meticulously copied by the artistic scribes and made available for everyone. Even the blind and illiterate Jews could hear them during worship services, when the ancient scrolls were unrolled and read to them.

The oral laws, however, were never written down or made available to anyone. Consequently, the Pharisees were able to veer away from original, written Jewish Scripture by focusing on the relatively exclusive, oral laws.

Their relaxation system worked as planned. The Jewish people began to ride the alluring waves of acceptance and prosperity, and the Pharisees were becoming more popular and influential.

The Sadducees, priests, and Essenes disagreed with the interpretations of the Pharisees. They considered the oral laws to be confusing, hampering, and controversial. They accused the Pharisees of compromising their Jewish faith and making it very difficult for godly Jews to live a holy life.

To give an example of changes that were made by the Pharisees, additions were made to "Thou shall not commit adultery," which made it unlawful to talk with or even look at women who were not their wives. The Pharisees themselves would lower their heads when passing by women, and if they ran right smack into a wall, they would wear their bruises very proudly! Because they ran into walls frequently, they were often called the "Bleeding Pharisees".

Scores of rules were made about observing the Sabbath day. Here are a few examples.

(1) A person could ride a donkey on Saturday without breaking any rules, but no one could carry a switch for speed, because he would be guilty of burdening an animal.

(2) A Pharisee could give money to a beggar on the Sabbath, but only if the beggar reached inside his house for it, because the Pharisee was not to reach outside.

(3) A man could rescue a bogged cow or sheep on the Sabbath but otherwise could not work.

(4) A boy couldn't wash his dog; a girl couldn't plait her hair; a woman couldn't look into a mirror or knead dough; and no one could peel fruit, light a fire, or put out a fire on the Sabbath.

Did the Pharisees know that they were leading the masses away from God? Absolutely not. They thought they were leading them to God with extra credit.

The Pharisees were pious Jews who certainly acknowledged a higher authority than the gods and goddesses of the Greco-Roman Empire. But they mistakenly thought they had to earn God's love and approval. Consequently, they purposefully altered His laws to make them more difficult. Since worship was always good, the Pharisees figured difficult worship would be even better, so God would love them more. They didn't admit their wrongs, because they never saw their wrongs. The Pharisees were earnest but lamentably misguided.

# 10
## The Escalation of Conflicts

Knowing the conflicts with the Jewish leaders were about to escalate, Jesus asked the four fishermen to become His permanent disciples. He said to them, "Come, follow me ... and I will make you fishers of men" (Matthew 4:19; Mark 1:17). Peter, Andrew, James, and John left their nets immediately and followed Jesus back to His new headquarters in Capernaum.

When the Sabbath came, Jesus began teaching His interpretations of Scripture in the synagogue. The people, as well as His primary disciples, were amazed, because His information, approach, and demeanor were so different from the rabbis' methods. "He taught them as one who had authority, not as the teachers of the law" (Matthew 1:22).

They were right! Jesus was His own authority, and the original words of God were very different from what they had heard before. His personal, direct, and intensive approach was also different from that of the studious rabbis and scribes, who based their authority on quotes from other teachers of God's laws.

Jesus introduced the people to the differences between the original laws, which God handed down through Moses, and the altered laws the Pharisees handed down through the rabbis by saying things like, "You have heard ... but I tell you," or, "It has been said ... but I tell you" (Matthew 5:21, 22, 31, 32).

The people were surprised and somewhat worried about His changes, so they asked Him if He had come to abolish their laws. Their question provided Jesus with His first opportunity to shed some light on one of the Pharisees' many wrongs. He answered that He had not come to abolish their laws at all but to fulfill them (Matthew 5:17).

That same day in the synagogue, a man possessed by an evil spirit started yelling at Jesus. Jesus sternly replied, "Be quiet ... Come out of him!" (Mark 1:25). The spirit was angry, but he also knew he was doomed (Mark 1:24). So he caused as much damage as possible by shaking the man violently before coming out of him with a shriek (Mark 1:26).

The witnesses were now doubly impressed. First, Jesus taught lessons with substantial information and established higher principles of God's laws. Then He demonstrated a supernatural ability to pull a demon out of a possessed man. "News about Him spread quickly over the whole region of Galilee" (Mark 1:28).

Demons, or evil spirits, are mentioned throughout the New Testament. They are not mythical creatures. They are fallen angels that joined Satan in rebellion against God. They are real beings and continue to oppose all righteousness. They knew Jesus was the Son of God and always recognized Him. They knew they would lose to him eventually (Matthew 8:29; Mark 1:24), but they continued to oppose Him anyway.

After the exorcism, Jesus left the synagogue in Capernaum and went to visit Peter's mother nearby, who was very sick with a fever. After healing her, the townspeople brought everyone they knew who was sick or possessed to Jesus. He healed many people and drove out more demons. He didn't let the demons speak, because they knew who He was (Mark 1:34), and it was too early for His true identity to be revealed. He needed more time to expose what was wrong with the political and religious systems of God's chosen people.

He left Capernaum for a little while and traveled through some smaller villages in Galilee with His four disciples to teach and heal many others. In a remote area, a man with leprosy found Jesus alone and begged Him to make him clean. Very compassionately, Jesus reached out, touched him, and said, "Be clean!" (Mark 1:41). The leprosy left the man immediately.

Knowing physical healings were rare in those days, Jesus asked the man not to tell anyone, because He didn't want His miracles to divert attention away from His messages. The man could not hold back his exuberance, though, so he announced the miracle to everyone who knew him. People flocked to Jesus. As a result, Jesus couldn't enter towns openly (Mark 1:45). Though He stayed outside in lonely places, people still came from everywhere.

A few days later, Jesus returned to Capernaum with His disciples. Some men brought a paralyzed friend there for Jesus to heal. They couldn't get near Him, however, because too many people were crowded around Him in the house. Undaunted by their dilemma, they carried their friend up onto the roof and removed enough slabs of clay to lower him on his mat to Jesus, who was standing right below them. Jesus was so impressed by their faith and ingenuity that He said to the paralytic, "Son, your sins are forgiven" (Mark 2:5).

In those days, people believed their lots in life were measures of God's approval and indications of the degree of their righteousness. The paralytic probably thought that he (or his parents) had done something to incur God's wrath and was consequently being punished for his sins. He would have welcomed having his sins forgiven by Jesus before being healed!

Not the Pharisees or scribes, though, who were present in the crowd that day. They firmly believed that God was the only One who could forgive sins (Mark 2:7; Luke 5:21), so they were astounded by Jesus' statement. They didn't voice their angry opinion that day, but they were *thinking* Jesus was a blasphemer. And Jesus read their minds.

They were right in knowing that only God can forgive sins (Isaiah 43:25) but wrong in thinking He was a blasphemer. They were about to learn who He really was! Their thoughts gave Him the opportunity to unveil His true identity, because the Pharisees were the only religious leaders who knew all the written and oral laws.

Jesus addressed them directly and asked why they were thinking such things. He asked, "Which would be easier to say to the paralytic, 'Your sins are forgiven' or … 'Get up, take your mat and walk'? (Mark 2:9).

Jesus didn't wait for their answer. Instead, He called Himself the Son of Man, which was a common prophetic term for the Messiah and then launched into His miracle. Looking first at the religious leaders and then at the paralytic, Jesus said, "But that you may know that the Son of Man has authority on earth to forgive sins … I tell you, get up, take your mat, and go home" (Mark 2:10–11).

To everyone's complete shock and awe, the paralytic did just that! Jesus' power to heal the man's severe infirmities proved the truth behind His messianic claims and thus, His authority to forgive sins. But it wasn't accepted.

The religious leaders clearly received Jesus' message to them, because they knew all about the Son of Man. The prophet Daniel first introduced the term when he wrote,

In my vision at night, I looked, and there before me was one like a son of man, coming with the clouds of heaven. He approached the Ancient of Days and was led into His presence. He was given authority, glory, and sovereign power; all peoples, nations, and men of every language worshiped him. His dominion is an everlasting dominion that will not pass away, and his kingdom is one that will never be destroyed. (Daniel 7:13, 14)

The religious leaders heard the assertions of Jesus, but they refused to acknowledge that His power came from God, or that He actually was God. They weren't ready for the Messiah, yet. They were doing just fine, thank you, on their own, so they didn't think they needed a Savior. They liked the status quo and their power over the people. They weren't about to relinquish their power to a carpenter from Nazareth. They were all ready to work overtime to disprove all His claims. If they could trap Him into saying something against God or Rome, they could report His blasphemy or treason to higher authorities, and His fate would be taken out of their hands.

Jesus knew their schemes and that this confrontation over healing the paralytic was the first of five early conflicts with the Pharisees. The next one came after He asked Matthew to become His fifth disciple and then dared to eat dinner with him and his friends.

Matthew was Jewish, but he collected taxes for Rome. The Jewish people hated tax collectors, because they had a bad reputation of charging more money than Caesar actually demanded. They became wealthy by pocketing the surplus for themselves. The Jews considered them to be great sinners.

When the Pharisees saw Jesus eating dinner with Matthew and his friends, they asked the disciples why Jesus ate with tax collectors and sinners. Jesus answered the Pharisees Himself, saying, "It is not the healthy who need a doctor, but the sick. I have not come to call the righteous, but sinners" (Mark 2:17).

The third conflict arose when the religious leaders asked Jesus why His disciples were not fasting when their disciples were, and some of John the Baptist's disciples were, also. In those days, many Orthodox Jews fasted twice every week (Luke 18:12), but Jesus thought that was too often and out of touch with reality. Jesus wanted His disciples to fast during stressful times of great need, like before a funeral. He didn't expect them to fast during celebrations. He told the Pharisees that there was no need for His disciples to mourn or fast while they were enjoying His presence. They could mourn and fast when He was taken from them, when He was crucified (Luke 2:20).

The fourth conflict was impactful. It set the stage for what God considered to be unlawful on the Sabbath day versus what the Pharisees considered to be unlawful. It occurred when Jesus allowed His hungry disciples to eat grain in the fields on the Sabbath. The Pharisees accused them of breaking the Sabbath laws.

Jesus disagreed. He knew that eating grain on the Sabbath was not unlawful in God's eyes. A farmer was not allowed to harvest his grain to sell for profit on the Sabbath, but a hungry man was always allowed to glean handfuls of a neighbor's grain to satisfy his immediate hunger (Deuteronomy 23:25). Therefore, Jesus defended His disciples against the Pharisees' charges. Furthermore, He reproached the Pharisees by sarcastically reminding them what King David had done when he was hungry (Mark 2:25). The Pharisees were experts of the Jewish Scriptures and should not have needed to be reminded of anything about King David.

As that story goes, when David and his companions were running for their lives from King Saul, they asked the priests for food. The high priest gave them their consecrated showbread, which had been set aside because it was holy.

This bread was actually twelve loaves of unleavened bread made from the finest flour. The loaves were placed before the Lord in two rows of six each on a table in the holy place within the tabernacle (and later, within the temple). The loaves represented the twelve tribes of Israel and symbolized the holiness of the entire nation, which had accepted the LORD as its one God Almighty. These loaves were replaced each Sabbath with fresh ones and were usually eaten only by the priests (Leviticus 24:5–9).

The priests didn't want David to starve, so they gave the holy bread to him and his companions (1 Samuel 21:1–6). God didn't want them to starve, either. Nor did He condemn them. He was merciful, because their survival was more important than their breaking of a ritual law. The *heart* of God's laws was always more important than precise adherence to them. This was a beautiful concept the Pharisees never seemed to grasp.

Knowing the Pharisees were rigid, merciless legalists, who upheld a strict set of their own laws, Jesus stood tall and declared publicly, "The Sabbath was made for man, not man for the Sabbath" (Mark 2:27).

"Sabbath" comes from a Hebrew word referring to rest or a ceasing of activity. God blessed His people with a day of rest each week, because He had rested on the seventh day after He created the world and all things in it. Rest for the people was necessary and mandatory. None of God's people—nor their children, servants, visitors, or animals—were to do any work on the seventh day (Exodus 20:8–11). They were supposed to worship God that day and be thankful for His creations and blessings. "If you keep your feet from breaking the Sabbath, and from doing as you please on my holy day, if you call the Sabbath a delight and the LORD'S holy day honorable, and if you honor it by not going your own way or speaking idle words, then you will find your joy in the LORD" (Isaiah 58:13–14).

God intended the Sabbath to be a "delight" for His people, but with their multiple laws, the Pharisees had changed it into a day of burdens. God's original commandments were designed for His glory and the benefit of His people. They were not burdensome. On the contrary. When they were woven together, they created a life that was structured, meaningful, and wholesome. His commandments would allow His people to live together as a healthy, peaceful nation under God.

The Pharisees were ruining God's intended blessings, and the people were losing their liberties and justices. Jesus intended to expose their selfish, ruling desires and to challenge their assumed authority. He knew that was a direct threat to their errant leadership, and He ignited His opposition of their regulations with two sizzling declarations.

(1) "I tell you that one greater than the temple is here" (Matthew 12:6).
(2) "So, the Son of Man is Lord even of the Sabbath" (Matthew 12:8; Mark 2:8; Luke 6:5).

In other words, Jesus told them having God dwell with them in person was far superior to God's dwelling place in Jerusalem, and God's presence gave Him the rank and prerogative to trump the Pharisees' man-made, Sabbatarian rule.

Was Jesus claiming Deity? Yes! He was effectively saying "I am God!" And every person there knew it. Some believed Him. Some didn't.

Most of the Pharisees believed Him, but they still wanted Him to assist them in their leadership. They thought they had their religious ducks in a row and were heading in the right direction, so they were irritated when Jesus didn't fall in line.

Nevertheless, the Pharisees accepted Jesus' challenge of their authority and continued to oppose Him, because they knew that the majority of the commoners could not read. The Pharisees thought they could hide the truth from the unbelievers and distort the truth from the believers just by saying, "No, he's not," every time Jesus said, "Yes, I am." The controversies would all become their ruling word against a challenger's word. And since the people didn't actually know what was written on the ancient scrolls, the Pharisees thought they had an edge. They were ready to butt heads.

Jesus did just that. He left the grain fields and went directly to the synagogue, where He found a man with a shriveled hand. Looking for a way to accuse Jesus of breaking a Sabbath law, the Pharisees asked Him, "Is it lawful to heal on the Sabbath?" (Matthew 12:10).

Jesus knew that the Pharisees prohibited the practice of medicine on the Sabbath unless the situation was life-threatening. But He also knew there were no written laws that forbade an act of mercy on the Sabbath. He refused to let the oral traditions of the Pharisees interfere with anyone's compassion for the needy, so He told them, "It is lawful to do good on the Sabbath" (Matthew 12:12). Jesus considered good deeds to *always* be lawful, especially on the Sabbath.

After answering the Pharisees' question, Jesus told the man to stretch out his hand for everyone to see. It had been completely restored (Matthew 12:13; Mark 3:5; Luke 6:10). The Pharisees were enraged. Not only had Jesus humiliated them in public by rejecting their laws, He then provocatively healed a man's hand on the Sabbath. They took their opposition of Jesus to a higher level. He was becoming a definite threat to their established religious hierarchy, so they went out and plotted how they might kill Him (Matthew 12:14).

# 11
## Formal Calling of the Disciples

Jesus knew about the vengeful plots of the Pharisees, and He knew the religious leaders would be successful in having Him killed. So He left the area to select His special core of disciples. It was time to begin training His advocates.

As disciples, or students, Jesus would teach them the differences between what God values and what the world values. He would teach them God's plan for humanity and demonstrate God's compassion for it. He didn't expect His disciples to grasp His true identity, His mission, or His concepts quickly. It would take them more than three years to comprehend who He really was and what their ultimate purpose in life would be.

As the disciples began to understand what Jesus said and did, He would empower them to teach and heal others in His name. Then He would send them out on their own as His apostles, or representatives. By doing this, Jesus would show the world that God can transfer His power to those who believe in His Son and want to extend His kingdom. The eventual showdown was going to be very exciting.

When Jesus left Capernaum, a large crowd from Galilee followed Him. Wanting to be alone for a while, He went up on a mountainside to pray and spent the night there. The next morning. He called His chosen twelve up to Him and asked them to accompany Him.

Every one of the disciples accepted His call. They knew He was a spokesman for God, and had His authority to teach Scripture and heal others. They knew He cared deeply for all of them. They didn't understand everything He said, but it didn't matter, because He had won their hearts. Jesus was unlike any man who had ever lived, so they left their trades and their families to follow Him permanently, without knowing or caring about hardships or duration.

These are the men whom Jesus called (Matthew 10:2–4; Mark 3:16–19; Luke 6:14–16).

Simon Peter
Andrew (Peter's brother)

James (son of Zebedee)
John (James's brother)
Matthew (tax collector)
Philip (Andrew's friend)
Bartholomew (aka Nathanael, friend of Philip)
Thomas ("doubting Thomas")
James (son of Alphaeus)
Simon the Zealot
Judas (Thaddaeus/aka Jude)
Judas Iscariot (who betrayed Jesus)

# 12
## The Sermon on the Mount

Jesus left with His disciples and continued to teach in the Galilean synagogues. His message never varied: "Repent, for the kingdom of heaven is near" (Matthew 4:17). He healed *every* sickness and disease of *all* the people who found their way to Him. News spread, crowds enlarged, and people flocked to Him from everywhere—from Galilee, Judea, Jerusalem, from every shore around Lake Galilee, and from Gentile regions east of the Jordan River, where the people worshipped multiple gods (Matthew 4:25). They all came to hear about a kingdom. Instead, they heard about a lifestyle, the lifestyle of those who would live in the kingdom. They were all perplexed, because the lifestyle was so different from the one they were living.

The twelve disciples were also confused. So Jesus pulled them aside and began to teach them about His new kingdom in much greater detail. This initial explanation was called the Sermon on the Mount, because it was first outlined and given on a mountain plateau. It was His longest recorded speech in Scripture (Matthew 5, 6, 7) and the greatest sermon given by the greatest Man who ever lived.

The sermon was confusing to those who heard it, because it was a presentation of a perfect life in a perfect world as seen through the eyes of God. It didn't resemble any way of life known to those in the Middle East. Jesus knew He would thoroughly explain the kingdom of God in the years to come, because it would always be His central theme. He wanted His disciples to see the whole picture before He taught them how to put the pieces together. He wanted to summarize all of His teachings for His disciples, so they would understand where they were going before He led the way. He wanted them to see the rainbow before they saw the storms.

Jesus began His sermon with the Beatitudes (from the Latin word *beatus,* meaning "blessed"). He announced, "Blessed are the poor in spirit … Blessed are those who mourn … Blessed are the meek … Blessed are those who hunger and thirst for righteousness" (Matthew 5:1–11). These beatitudes were not given as a prescription to make

God happy. They were given as invitations to open up the kingdom of God for everyone.

The Pharisees taught heaven was only open for healthy, influential, pious, Jewish males. They considered the worldly treasures of the wealthy, successful, or powerful Jewish citizens to be indications that they or their parents had somehow earned God's approval, so their possessions and privileges were merely God's rewards for their righteousness. The Pharisees never thought of themselves as sinners who needed a Savior. On the contrary, they thought of themselves as holy favorites on their way to heaven.

Jesus fervently disagreed, and lashed out at them with three dire warnings.

"Woe to you who are rich, for you have already received your comfort" (Luke 6:24). The Pharisees were physically and spiritually rich, or so they thought. But their riches were going to end in this world. They would not carry to the next.

"Woe to you who are well fed now, for you will go hungry" (Luke 6:25). The Pharisees knew Scripture backward and forward, so they were spiritually well-fed. But because they weren't teaching all of it as it was originally written, they were going to lose that knowledge, also. They were not going to understand the fulfillment of prophecies carried out by Jesus, because God was going to hide it from them. They were going to become spiritually lean.

"Woe to you when all men speak well of you" (Luke 6:26). The Pharisees were respected by men but not by God.

Jesus couldn't convince the Pharisees that they needed a Savior, so He couldn't hold their attention with His messages. He could, however, always attract the downtrodden who still loved hearing Him say, "Come to me, all you who are weary and burdened, and I will give you rest" (Matthew 11:28).

Most of the poor and downtrodden had always been poor in spirit, because they never dreamed they would ever be able to enter the kingdom of God. They wanted to do what God wanted them to do. They hungered for righteousness, but they thought they had been bypassed. They didn't know the true words of God because they couldn't read, so they relied on their religious leaders to teach them, without realizing they were being misled. They loved their invitation from Jesus, and learning what God really said about the people they were going to find in heaven. They were relieved to know everyone there would be humble and considerate of others. They were flabbergasted, though, when Jesus told them the Pharisees would not be there.

Wait a minute! God was *not* going to bless the religious leaders who represented the epitome of righteousness to the Jewish people? That's right, He was not!

Why not? Because the Pharisees were primarily responsible for relaxing God's original laws in order to help Jewish citizens blend into the foreign, pagan lifestyles surrounding them. God disapproved. He did not want His chosen people to blend in with any foreigners. He wanted them to resist foreign ways and stand out for *His* ways. He wasn't about to lower any of His standards to accommodate their sins. God's laws were holy, right, and thoughtful of all humans. The Pharisees' laws were trivial, wrong, and meaningless. Consequently, the Pharisees would not be blessed, and neither would the people—unless they raised their moral and ethical standards above those of their proud, religious leaders. This concept was the major theme in the Sermon on the Mount: "For, I tell you that unless your righteousness surpasses that of the Pharisees and the teachers of the law, you will certainly not enter the kingdom of heaven" (Matthew 5:20).

No way! How could commoners possibly rise above the righteousness of their religious leaders? (1) By realizing they were barreling down a road that was heading over a steep cliff. (2) By trusting Jesus and His messages, whether they understood them or not. It's why Jesus came to earth … to save people by exposing the dangers of the wrong road and leading them to the securities of the right road. "Trust in the Lord with all your heart and lean not on your own understanding. In all your ways, acknowledge Him, and He will make your paths straight" (Proverbs 3:5–6).

Jesus knew that the Pharisees were in a nosedive. They had started out as the biblical fundamentalists of their day. They had been very powerful, repentant, charitable, and kind, but their increasing appetite for dominance changed their hearts. As extremely popular religious leaders, they gained full control over the social and political aspects of Jewish life. They gradually became the most powerful influence in Judea. No empire could rule Palestine without the support of the Pharisees, and the Pharisees knew it. Their rise to such power fostered arrogance and feelings of exclusive superiority. They developed tremendous egos and wanted to impress people with their "connections" to God. They turned their faith into performances. They strapped boxes containing Scripture (phylacteries) to their head or upper arm and prayed grandiosely on popular street corners or in marketplaces. When they made short, sacrificial fasts, they wore gaunt, hungry looks, as if they were starving. They liked to be acknowledged, so they had trumpets herald their donations to the needy. The Pharisees were definitely not into anonymity!

By the time the Romans controlled Palestine in 63 BC, the Pharisees had degenerated into empty, unprincipled legalists, all in the mighty, mighty shroud of "religion." Unprincipled? Yes. They were no longer restrained by fundamental truths or any motivating forces of right and wrong. Differentiations became cloudy. What the Pharisees *said* was not what they felt or did. They preached "love one another" but continued to allow poor people to be oppressed. They were quick to judge people as sick, unclean, criminal, or outcast. And they avoided them instead of reaching out to help them.

Empty? Yes. By focusing on legalistic trivialities instead of mercy, justice, and faithfulness, the Pharisees changed Judaism from a fulfilling life of loving God and one another to an empty life of striving to follow insignificant laws.

Jesus came to change that. He knew the Pharisees cared more about their superiority than the well-being of their people. He called them hypocrites more than once. They were living for appearance instead of humbly for God. The people had been fooled by the Pharisees' fake behavior, and Jesus intended to expose them for who they really were. The truth would set His followers free. It would also get Him killed, but that was part of His mission. The people had been misled by their religious leaders, but Jesus would free them to choose their own destinies—life for God or life for themselves.

Jesus explained to His disciples that the Pharisees were teaching laws God had not designed for His people. Jesus gave them examples of the laws that were currently being taught in the synagogues and then countered them with God's original laws, which Moses and the prophets had written down. For instance, Jesus said, "You have heard that it was said: 'Love your neighbor and hate your enemy.' But I tell you: Love your enemies and pray for those who persecute you" (Matthew 5:43–44). Jesus knew that "hate your enemy" could not be found in any of the Old Testament writings. On the contrary, good things were supposed to be done for enemies (Proverbs 25:21). "Hate your enemy" was actually a false doctrine drawn up by the Pharisees and scribes from Leviticus 19:18, which commanded the opposite: "Do not seek revenge or bear a grudge against one of your people, but love your neighbor as yourself."

None of Jesus' countering truths in the Sermon on the Mount were new. He had not come to earth to change or abolish any of the original laws. He came to fulfill, or complete them (Matthew 5:17). He would teach the original laws correctly and obey them perfectly. He gave several other examples of false doctrines being taught (Matthew 5:21, 27, 31, 33, 38) before continuing to reprove the Pharisees for other poor tactics of leadership.

The Pharisees not only taught the wrong laws, they also demonstrated the wrong behavior. So Jesus continued to target their shortcomings. If He could lower the esteem held for them by the godly Jews, all the people would then realize that the bogus "righteousness of the Pharisees" really could be surpassed.

God wasn't fooled by the rituals of the Pharisees. He considered their external righteousness to be nothing more than worthless self-righteousness. They were praying, fasting, and making public donations to impress others, not to please God. Jesus knew people's feelings, or inner attitudes of heart, are always more meaningful to God than any outward expressions of obedience. Therefore, He taught His disciples to pray privately, fast privately, and give donations anonymously. "Then your Father, who sees what is done in secret, will reward you" (Matthew 6:4, 6, 18).

Jesus wanted His disciples to spend their lives collecting God's rewards for learning His will and continually trying to walk in His ways. Those rewards are far greater than anything they could ever receive from family, friends, or society. They are worth collecting, because they are everlasting treasures in heaven. They cannot be stolen or destroyed, so they are much more valuable than any material possessions or treasures on earth. Jesus never denounced worldly goods, but He wanted to make sure they were not anyone's first priorities! Money is not the root of evil, but the *love* of money is (1 Timothy 6:10). The first priority of Jesus' followers would always be to please God, "for where your treasure is, there will be your heart, also" (Matthew 6:21).

What is the best way to store treasures for the kingdom of heaven? By looking for ways to quietly help others. Why? Because how we treat others in this world determines how we will be treated in the next.

The Sermon on the Mount introduced the possibility of living in a troubled world with a surreal sense of inner peace, regardless of frightening events, misfortunes, sorrows, or illnesses. There were no guarantees against pain, loss, grief, or shame, but Jesus promised God would always take care of people who sought His kingdom and His righteousness. None of them would have to worry about basic things like food, water, or what might happen tomorrow. All of them would receive God's promises.

(1) Ask for His help, and it will be given.
(2) Seek His kingdom, and it will be found.
(3) Knock on the door of His kingdom, and it will be opened (Matthew 7:7).

In other words, Jesus wanted the people to learn God's will through Him. Then He wanted them to try to walk in His ways—and always keep trying. God promised to help them turn from doing something wrong if they learned to recognize it, confess it, be genuinely sorry for it, and ask Him to help them turn toward what is right. That series of actions is called repentance. It is not only necessary for entering the kingdom; it is mandatory.

Would God's kingdom be easy to enter? Absolutely not. "Small is the gate and narrow the road that lead to life, and only a few find it" (Matthew 7:14). It's hard for humans to do what's right. It's easier to do what's popular. It's difficult to live for God and others. It goes directly against selfish, human nature. It's easier to follow people who accept a few wrongs, especially when they are religious leaders. God understands human tendencies. It's why He promised to help those who humbly ask for His assistance.

Jesus warned His disciples that there would always be false prophets like the Pharisees, teaching false doctrines in the world. His chosen Twelve were to be on guard and to watch out for them. False prophets were wolves in sheep's clothing, but they could be readily recognized by their "bad fruit," their bad characteristics of pride, arrogance, greed, selfishness, and so on. Anyone who lives for his or her own pleasure will always display bad fruit.

In contrast, good fruit is the fruit of the Spirit. It is displayed as "love, joy, peace, patience, kindness, goodness, faithfulness, gentleness, and self-control" (Galatians 5:22). Jesus expected His followers to be dramatically different from the majority of people around them. He would empower them to exercise discipline and grace, and stand out for what is right.

Who are the few who will find the kingdom of God? The wise ones who accept the words of Jesus as truth and put them into practice by thinking good thoughts, using kind words, and looking for ways to help others. Random acts of kindness. These wise ones are like builders who build their houses on rock-solid foundations. They will survive the storms and live blessed lives. The majority of others who reject His words and fail to put them into practice are compared to foolish builders, who build their houses on shifting sand (Matthew 7:26; Luke 6:49).

Jesus knew He had squeezed a lot of lofty concepts into one sermon and had confused His disciples about the new lifestyle He wanted them to adopt. But He would serve as their role model for the next three years and gradually help them absorb His principles, values, and beliefs.

Why didn't Jesus just tell them who He was instead of telling them how God wanted them to live their lives? Because He wanted His disciples to develop strong convictions about what they were doing, instead of dissolving into quivering little figures of mush.

If Jesus had revealed His identity to nonbelievers at this stage of His mission, they would have locked Him up as a crazy person, or killed Him outright for what they considered to be blatant blasphemy. It was too early for Him to die. He needed more time to expose what was wrong and demonstrate what was right.

If Jesus had revealed His identity to His disciples, they would have been overwhelmed by such an early statement of deity and remained weak in His presence. He wanted them to grow strong in their beliefs and become leaders in His absence.

# 13
## Reservations

After the Sermon on the Mount, Jesus and His permanent disciples continued traveling through Galilee, where He resumed His messages of the kingdom and upscaled His miracles. He wanted His miracles and discernments to convince the people of His authority and His link to God the Father. Knowing they would give credential weight to His messages, He increased His wonders and gradually began to reveal His true identity. At first, the people were likely to interpret them as prophetic and then ultimately understand them as divine. One day ... one future day ... the whole world would believe what He said and know He was exactly who He said He was. "As surely as I live, says the Lord, every knee will bow before me, every tongue will confess to God" (Romans 14:11; Isaiah 45:23).

Jesus realized He was introducing a kingdom that was different from the political or military kingdom people expected, and a lifestyle radically different from the ones they were living. He wanted them to commit their lives to an invisible world—the kingdom of heaven—and challenged them to live a lifestyle worthy of it. Most of the crowds were not interested. His kingdom was too confusing. Success seemed to involve a complete reversal of their values, such as,

Blessed are the poor in spirit.
Blessed are those who mourn.
Blessed are the meek.
Blessed are those who are persecuted. (Matthew 5)

Jesus seemed to be giving perplexing advice. He repetitively told crowds things like,

(1) Give to everyone who asks, and give secretly.
(2) Only God needs to know what you do for others.
(3) Your integrity can be measured by what you do when no one is looking.

(4) Love your enemy and pray for those who persecute you.

(5) Take no revenge. Turn the other cheek.

(6) Let God take care of the injustices that come your way.

(7) You don't need the approval of humans. You only need the approval of God. (Matthew 5–7)

Small wonder very few people were willing to commit their lives to Jesus! The demands of His kingdom were too high, the rewards were too vague, and their existing status in this world was not guaranteed in the next. The crowds continued to follow Jesus because His miracles were awesome, but few people had any interest in signing up for His strange kingdom.

Jesus understood all their reservations, but He wanted to change their convictions, lifestyles, and destinies. So He kept on preaching and teaching. He knew that most of the multitudes were living unfair and unfulfilled lives. He wanted them to find new joys in a new way of life … in the great search for the kingdom of God. He wanted them to crawl behind the eyes of God and see life from His perspective.

Jesus knew if the people changed their lives to please God instead of merely pleasing themselves, God would reward them generously. Even better, the more they tried to please Him, the more He would bless them. The cycle of greater resolve, greater rewards, and greater joys would snowball. By combining their world of despair with God's spiritual world of promises, they could effectively create a miniature realm of heaven on earth, because His blessings would stay with them. "Thy kingdom come, thy will be done, on earth as it is in heaven" (Matthew 6:10).

This little piece of heaven on earth would manifest in the joys of the people who realize God is in charge of all their circumstances and turmoils—not themselves, not the politicians, and not their religious leaders. These joys would not be the carefree joys of walking on worldly "easy street," but the profound joys of having God in their lives to love, lead, encourage, support, and help them live above their circumstances. They would then understand the true treasures of heaven and gain a calming sense of inner peace, peace with God, peace with others, and peace with themselves. Their lives would become fulfilling and very much worth living. It's what Jesus wanted for His followers … a spiritual world residing in their hearts. It's what God the Father wants for the whole world, a kingdom providing a little piece of heaven in the here and now and a wonderful hope for the new world to come, when He makes all things right and takes all rule away from Satan forever.

# 14
## Beelzebub

Jesus had His work cut out for Himself and a long way to go before He could turn things around for the weary people. His messages were beginning to fall on deaf ears, so He intensified His public displays in order to keep the crowds coming to learn more about His new kingdom. He wanted everyone to be part of it, so He set out to convince the masses, the leaders, and the Gentiles of His supreme authority and His link with God the Father.

Jesus began this new initiative by announcing in public, "All things have been committed to me by my Father. No one knows the Son except the Father, and no one knows the Father except the Son, and those to whom the Son chooses to reveal" (Matthew 11:27). Anyone who accepted His messages and His link to God the Father automatically became part of His new kingdom. It was out there for everyone! All they had to do was come, seek, knock, and trust.

The Pharisees had their work cut out for them, also. They didn't want the crowds to be enamored by Jesus or His miracles, so they set out with higher resolve to disprove everything that Jesus tried to prove.

Their first challenge arose when Jesus healed a demon-possessed man, who was also blind and mute. It was an amazing miracle and made many people wonder if Jesus might be the Son of David, after all (Matthew 12:23). Son of David and Son of God were the most common titles used for the coming Messiah. They stemmed from God's promise to King David that one of his descendants would be His Son, the Son of God: "I will be his father, and he will be my son" (2 Samuel 7:14). God's Son would be fully human and fully God.

When the Pharisees saw the people leaning toward Jesus, they tried to turn that tide by declaring His power came from Satan, not from God: "It is only by Beelzebub, the prince of demons, that this fellow drives out demons" (Matthew 12:24). To back them up, the teachers of the Law came down from Jerusalem and spread the same false claims: "He is possessed by Beelzebub! By the prince of demons, He is driving out demons" (Mark 3:22).

Beelzebub was a variation of *Baal-zebub,* which was a disdainful Hebrew term meaning "lord of the flies." Baal-zebub was the Philistine storm god who controlled disease brought by flies. Jesus and the religious leaders clearly used both terms in reference to Satan.

The Pharisees knew their statement was the exact opposite of the truth, but their influence and their jobs were at risk. Their primary obligation to Rome was to keep the volatile Israelites in line (*Pax Romana*). They worried that messianic frenzies would lead to an uprising against Roman occupation and oppression, which would be brutally crushed. The protectors would all be killed, and the Jewish leaders would be stripped of their power, allowances, and kickbacks. Heaven forbid! The Pharisees were determined to keep that from happening.

Lamentably, to save their place and their nation (John 11:48), the pious leaders committed the ultimate, unpardonable sin. They condemned themselves by saying that what was of God was of the Devil. It was a direct blasphemy against the Holy Spirit, and it would never be forgiven (Mark 3:28, 29).

Jesus told the people that the claims of the Pharisees couldn't possibly be true, because His miracles were always merciful, kind, and righteous. They were always performed to please God (Matthew 12:25–29; Luke 11:17–22). On the other hand, Satan's power would always be used against the righteous.

Jesus knew that the religious leaders had officially rejected His messages and His ministry, so He deliberately turned away from them. There was nothing more He could do. He had offered enough proof for all the religious leaders to know He was who He said He was, but they brushed Him aside. When Jesus turned away from the Pharisees, His disciples turned with Him. They didn't know exactly who they were following, but it didn't matter. They knew they were going in the right direction.

The multitudes, though, vacillated. They couldn't understand how Jesus could be their Messiah if their religious leaders had rejected Him. So they didn't make any commitments. They didn't yet understand Jesus had not come to earth as the Messiah of the world under the rules of Romans, the Pharisees, or any other visible superpower. He had come to be the Messiah of a new world ruled only by God.

Few people understood Jesus' ministry or mission, because the Pharisees continually bucked His authority and thwarted His objectives every step of the way. Jesus had to stop their deceptions. To counteract such interference from the religious leaders, Jesus started defining the kingdom of God by using parables, which were simple stories that taught one main point. God blocked the Pharisees from being able to understand the spiritual significance of the stories.

# 15
## Parables

Jesus used familiar themes in His parables, because they held everyone's attention and would be easy to remember. He talked about farmers, seeds, plants, droughts, good soil, bad soil, landlords (owners), and tenants (laborers). Most of His parables were intended to be mirrors for those who heard them. They helped the people recognize and understand themselves. They also helped them know God's heart and mind. They exposed human nature for what it was. And they brought encouragement by illuminating divine remedies.

Though the stories were always quite simple, the concepts weren't simple at all. They were spiritual truths that usually required explanations. Jesus personally explained them to His disciples when He was alone with them, and the Holy Spirit revealed the new truths to the few people in the crowds who were genuinely interested in learning more about the kingdom of God.

The Pharisees and anyone else who continually opposed Jesus would not be further enlightened about the kingdom. They would be spiritually blinded by their unbelief and wouldn't understand the parables.

That's why Jesus started teaching in parables after the Pharisees confused the crowds of people by telling them His power came from Satan. He knew they wouldn't be able to further mislead the people by mocking or scoffing at His messages if they didn't understand the spiritual truths behind them.

When the disciples asked Jesus why He was speaking to people in parables, He told them that spiritual comprehension is a gracious gift from God and not given to everyone. He told them, "The knowledge of the secrets of the kingdom of heaven has been given to you, but not to them" (Matthew 13:11). Jesus further explained that He was intentionally fulfilling Isaiah's prophecy to people who consistently refused to believe the words of God: "Be ever hearing, but never understanding; be ever seeing, but not perceiving" (Isaiah 6:9). The hearts of unbelievers would be calloused, their ears would be dull, and their eyes would be closed (Isaiah 6:10). Those who brushed aside His messages would lose what little understanding they thought they had (Matthew 13:12; Luke 8:18). On the other hand, those who tried to apply God's words to their daily lives would be rewarded with further understanding and wisdom.

Some scholars today think Jesus knew the Pharisees had condemned themselves by attributing the credentials of heaven to hell, so He consequently started teaching in parables to veil the truth, which protected them from suffering greater torment in eternity without Him. Just as there are various awards given in heaven for amounts of righteousness (Daniel 12:1–3; 1 Corinthians 3:10–15; 2 Corinthians 5:10), there are also various punishments given in hell for amounts of unrighteousness (Revelation 20:11–15; Matthew 11:22–24; Luke 12:47, 48; Hebrews 10:29, 30). Judicial blinding by speaking in parables just might have been an act of mercy toward the Pharisees to prevent more severe punishments in the future.

Of the forty or so parables recorded in the New Testament, the parable of the sower (Matthew 13:3–23) serves as a backdrop or setting for all of Jesus' parables. It reveals that productivity is always dependent on believing and receiving.

Everyone in Israel knew that seeds could be sown there either before or after plowing, because the rocky soil was not very deep. Productivity, however, was always unpredictable, because rainfall was irregular and often inadequate. Productivity was always dependent on the preparation of the soil and on belief or unbelief.

Seeds falling on fertile ground was equivalent to God's words falling on ears that could hear. Farming depended on what the farmers believed and how they applied it to their lives. When farmers asked God for rain, He expected them to believe in His ability to deliver it. And He expected them to have a hoe in their hands! He expected them to work with their hands, so their daily lives would win the respect of others, and so they would not be dependent on anyone else (1 Thessalonians 4:11, 12). If His people believed in Him enough to learn His will and consistently try to walk in His ways, He would always reward them.

Other parables were woven throughout the Gospels to answer specific questions or address particular situations in first-century Palestine. They all centered on belief in Jesus' authority and messages.

# 16
## A Royal Premiere for the Disciples

As Jesus and His disciples approached the small town of Nain, southeast of Nazareth, they came upon a funeral procession. Jewish funerals were normally held on the day of a death, because keeping a dead body overnight was thought to make a house unclean. A widow's only son had died. Jesus felt sorry for her, because she had lost her only means of support and care. He touched the coffin and said, "Young man, I say to you, get up" (Luke 7:14). The dead man sat up and began to talk.

The large crowd was amazed and filled with great respect for Jesus. They realized that He had the same God-given ability of Elijah and Elisha, who were two of their leading Old Testament prophets. Both of them had also brought dead sons back to life (1 Kings 17:17–24; 2 Kings 4:8–37). The crowd praised God for sending another true prophet.

Everyone knew that the prophets had fallen silent after Malachi. No one had heard God's voice for four hundred years. Rumors were spreading about a miracle worker who claimed to have the authority to speak for God, and this miracle convinced the crowd the rumors were true. "A great prophet has appeared among us … God has come to help His people" (Luke 7:16). His truth was marching on! News about Jesus continued to spread. The multitudes were still confused about the kingdom He proclaimed, but they were beginning to waver between enthusiastic support and outright rejection of Him.

John the Baptist was still in prison, but he had heard all the reports, too. He sent his disciples to Jesus to confirm whether He was the true Messiah. John had baptized Jesus and pronounced Him to the world as the Son of God (John 1:34). He had not lost faith in Him at all, but he couldn't believe the reports that Jesus was encountering unbelief and hostility, so he wanted His personal reassurance. Jesus sent John's disciples back to him with the encouraging reply that He was doing precisely what Scripture foretold about the Messiah: "Go back and report to John what you have seen and heard: The blind receive sight, the lame walk, those who have leprosy are cured, the deaf hear, the dead are raised, and the good news is preached to the poor. Blessed is the man who does not fall away on account of me" (Luke 7:22, 23). These were messianic promises quoted from Isaiah 35:5, 6 and Isaiah 61:1. Jesus knew John's faith was great, and he would not fall away. He didn't need to say anything more.

When Jesus saw more crowds gathering, He gave orders to leave Galilee and take a boat across to the other side of the lake, which was much less populated. No towns or villages existed along the narrow, eastern shore of Lake Galilee (Sea of Galilee), because cliffs rise up several thousand feet from near the water's edge. Jesus was tired and needed to rest. He also welcomed more time to spend alone with His disciples. He needed to broaden their horizons.

Without warning, a furious storm came up while they were out on the lake. Sudden, violent storms are common there between May and October, because the lake is seven hundred feet below sea level, and strong winds sweep through the northern and eastern gorges between cliffs. Waves crashed over the boat and terrified the disciples. They woke Jesus, crying out, "Lord, save us! We're going to drown!" (Matthew 8:25).

Jesus got up, rebuked the wind, and commanded the waves: "Quiet! Be still!" (Mark 4:39) Much to the amazement of the disciples, the storm abated, and the lake became completely calm. Jesus matter-of-factly asked them, "Why are you so afraid? Do you still have no faith?" (Mark 4:40). "Afraid" didn't even scratch the surface of how they felt! They had been terrified by the storm and astounded by His power over it. "Who is this? Even the winds and the waves obey Him!" (Mark 4:41). They knew He was a true prophet, who had the authority to speak for God. They also knew He was empowered by God, because they had seen Him heal the sick and raise the dead. But were there no limits? They knew God could still the waves of a surging sea (Psalm 89:9), but Jesus couldn't be God, because God was a Spirit. Jesus was a human who nearly slept through the raging storm because He had been so tired. They were completely bewildered.

The disciples were in for more astonishment the next day, when they landed on the eastern shore in the region of the Gerasenes (also referred to as the country of the Gadarenes). When Jesus got out of the boat, a demon-possessed man ran to Him from the tombs. The tombs were caves in the nearby hillsides used for burial chambers. They were also common dwelling places for the demented in those days.

Jesus knew the man was in tremendous agony. He had been crying out in unearthly screams for days and nights and cutting himself with sharp rocks. People had tried to subdue him with chains and irons on his hands and feet. But he had broken all of them, because he had been fortified with the strength of the demons.

When he fell on his knees in front of Jesus, Jesus distinguished the tormented man from the demon who possessed him and demanded the evil spirit to come out (Mark 5:8). The evil spirit responded, "What do you want with me, Jesus, Son of the Most High God? Swear to God that you won't torture me" (Mark 5:7). "Most High God" was a title used by both the Jews and the Gentiles to distinguish the God of Israel from all the lesser, pagan gods (Genesis 14:18–20; Numbers 24:16; Deuteronomy 32:8; Isaiah 14:14; Luke 1:32). All the evil spirits knew exactly who Jesus was, and they knew their fates (Matthew 8:29; Mark 1:24). They didn't try to change it. They merely tried to postpone it.

Jesus asked the demon for his name, and he said, "My name is Legion, for we are many" (Mark 5:9). "Legion" was a well-known Latin word that defined a Roman military unit of four to six thousand infantrymen. It implied that the poor man was controlled by a huge number of evil spirits, something not known by anyone else before Jesus asked its name.

The demons knew that Jesus had the authority and power to bind them and send them into the underworld, where they would be held for final judgment (2 Peter 2:4; Jude 6), so they begged Him not to send them out of the Gentile area. They asked to be sent instead into a herd of pigs, which were grazing on a hillside nearby. Jesus granted His permission. When they came out of the man and entered the pigs, "the herd, about two thousand in number, rushed down the steep bank into the lake and were drowned" (Mark 5:13).

The herdsmen rushed into both town and countryside to report what had happened. The residents then hurried back to the scene. They took one look at the calm man they knew had been demented, and they listened to other witnesses who confirmed the herdsmen's stories. Then they pleaded with Jesus to leave their region.

These Gadarenes were not Jewish. If any of them had been Jewish at one time, they no longer had any regard for the Mosaic laws of cleanliness. Godly Jews would not have lived near large herds of pigs, because they considered them to be unclean animals.

The residents were non-Jews, but they certainly had respect for the God of Israel. Everybody did! They also had respect for the traveling miracle worker and reputed prophet named Jesus. His healing miracles would have been welcomed in their region, but His display of enormous spiritual power was disruptive, costly, and overwhelming. So He was asked to leave. The residents were worried about what He might do if He were allowed to stay.

Jesus understood their reaction and was not insulted by their request. He would have liked to heal their illnesses and spread the good news about His new kingdom of heaven on earth, but as it was, He left in good standing and knew He had gained many strong witnesses of His abilities.

As Jesus was getting back into His boat, the man who had formerly been possessed by evil spirits begged to join Him and His disciples. Jesus denied his earnest request but asked him to return to his family and relate what the Lord had done for him (Mark 5:18). His family lived in another Gentile area nearby, known as the Decapolis. It was a collection of ten Hellenized cities east of the Jordan River, and Jesus needed their support also. He knew He would travel there within the next year, and it was always good for His reputation to precede Him!

The man respectfully obliged. He announced what Jesus had mercifully done for him, "and all the people were amazed" (Mark 5:20).

The return trip to Galilee must have been profoundly sobering for the disciples. In the past few days, Jesus had demonstrated His awesome power to them over death, over the natural world of weather and nature, and over the supernatural world of spirits. He didn't stand up in the boat to remind them what He had done. He didn't have to. They had seen His upscaled miracles with their own eyes, and their faith in Him was leap-frogging. They did not know that He was the Son of God, yet, but they did know that He was far more than a mere mortal. Their horizons had definitely been enlarged.

When Jesus crossed back over the lake, another large crowd gathered around Him. Jairus, one of the synagogue leaders, fell at His feet. His daughter was dying, and he begged Jesus to come back to his house with him to heal her.

Jesus was following Jairus when a sick woman touched His clothes, knowing that He could heal her, too. She had been suffering from some type of chronic internal hemorrhaging for twelve years and was embarrassed by her abnormal blood loss. It not only weakened her but left her ceremonially "unclean," so she had been excluded from both the synagogue and the temple in Jerusalem. Everyone shunned her, because anyone she touched also became "unclean" for one full day (Leviticus 15:25–27).

The woman knew Jesus could cure her, but she didn't want to touch Him or draw any attention to herself. So she touched His garment and was healed instantly. No one in the crowd was aware of the miracle, but Jesus instantly knew that power had been drawn from Him. He turned around and asked, "Who touched my clothes?" (Mark 5:30). He must have asked kindly and lessened the fear that the woman had about being revealed, because she came to Him, fell at His feet, and told Him the whole story.

Jesus told her that her faith in Him had healed her, because there was nothing magical about His clothes. He wanted her to know that faith alone doesn't heal. He does! She was healed because she came to Him and was truthful.

While Jesus was speaking to the woman, some men came out from Jairus's house and told him to stop bothering Jesus, because his daughter was dead. Jesus immediately comforted Jairus by telling him, "Don't be afraid; just believe" (Mark 5:36). Jesus wanted Jairus to keep the same faith he had in coming to Him in the first place. With that little bit of encouragement, Jesus walked into Jairus's house and invited Peter, James, and John to come in with them.

The house was very noisy. The traditional mourners and flute players had already arrived. As mentioned earlier, Jewish people were buried the same day they died. Public mourning was not allowed after a burial, so the funeral arrangements were carried out quickly. Professional mourners were hired to wail plaintively while reciting the name of the departed one and anyone else who had died recently. People would hear the mourners and the music and come to comfort the family.

When Jesus walked in, He prophesied that the girl was not dead but merely asleep, and He sent all the people away (Matthew 9:24). The crowd of mourners turned into a crowd of derisive hecklers, who laughed at Jesus and His apparently absurd statement as they left the house.

Jesus wasn't fazed by their mockery. He led Peter, James, John, and the parents into the daughter's room. He held her hand and said, "Little girl, I say to you, get up" (Mark 5:41). The little twelve-year-old stood up immediately and walked around (Mark 5:42).

Jesus knew she would be hungry, so He thoughtfully told her parents to get her something to eat. He also told them not to announce His miracle right away. He needed time to escape from any angry opponents who might try to kill Him after hearing about another resurrection.

# 17
## Second Rejection in Nazareth

Jesus and His disciples returned to the region near Nazareth where He had grown up. He had begun His mission there with an announcement of His intentions. And He was nearly killed by His hometowners after warning them not to follow in the fateful paths of their ancestors, who had rejected the words of God.

Jesus wanted to see if their disbelief had diminished. It had not. The Nazarenes acknowledged His wisdom and the miracles they had heard about, but they rejected His claims that He was the fulfillment of all the messianic prophecies. Empowered by God? Yes! Prophet? Yes! Messiah? No way! He couldn't be the Son of God for crying out loud. He was Mary's boy. He was a local carpenter who lived down the road. He was the brother of James, Joseph, Judas, and Simon (Mark 6:3). He was one of them. What was He thinking?

Jesus was disappointed in their poor attempt to cover their aversion to spiritual repentance. After all He had said and done since His first mission there the previous year, He was amazed by their lack of faith in Him. He sadly told them, "Only in his hometown, among His relatives and in his own house, is a prophet without honor" (Mark 6:5; Matthew 13:57).

He left Nazareth after healing a few people by laying His hands on them. He never returned.

# 18
## From Disciples to Apostles

When Jesus called His disciples to follow Him permanently, He stayed right with them as their role model. They were His students. (The word "disciple" emphasizes learning and following.) He taught them the good news about the kingdom of God. He revealed how their religious leaders were leading them away from God's benevolent intentions for humankind. He exposed what was wrong in discussions with them and demonstrated what was right through His miracles. He taught them how to honor God and respect others. He wanted them to use their new wisdom for the benefit of others, because how they treated others in this world would determine how they would be treated in the next.

When Jesus became convinced that His disciples understood why He said what He said and did what He did, He would empower them to teach Scripture, heal illnesses, and drive out demons—all in His name. Finally, He would send them out on their own missions as His apostles, His representatives. The word "apostle" means "one who is sent out." It emphasizes delegated authority.

Jesus wanted His nation of Israel to know that He could extend His authority and power through His apostles. If the religious leaders viewed Him as a thorn in their side, just wait until they saw what twelve of His empowered representatives could do!

The apostles' messages would be far more important than their miracles, because they would teach the people that the King was actually here on earth, but the arrival of His full kingdom would depend on Israel's reception of Jesus as the promised One, ushering in a new era.

What was this message of the apostles? It was the same one proclaimed by both John the Baptist and Jesus. John the Baptist preached, "Repent, for the kingdom of heaven is near" (Matthew 3:2). Jesus preached, "The time has come … the kingdom of God is near. Repent, and believe the good news" (Mark 1:15).

Yes, repentance was necessary to gain the new lifestyle Jesus was promoting. Turning from ample to humble would not be easy for anyone, but it would be well worth the effort, because God promised everlasting joy in the long run would transcend any acquiescence.

The "good news" (gospel) was that God knew humans are not able to overcome sin by themselves. So He sent Jesus to overcome it for them. Consequently, they would not be separated from God when they died. This good news gave all people a choice. Those who believed Jesus and accepted His instructions would enter the kingdom of God. Those who continually rejected Him would not. In other words, those who changed their lives and started living to please God would know an everlasting life of joy. Those who continued living life to please themselves would not.

Jesus knew the Israelites did not fully understand the principles of the new kingdom, but that wouldn't prevent them from entering it. Those who wanted to learn about it would learn and try to apply it to their lives. All they had to do was trust Him enough to take the initial baby steps toward living their lives to please God. Taking a small step forward would be like planting a mustard seed and watching it grow. They would be handsomely rewarded for following His instructions and quickly realize the infinite wisdom behind His words. They would naturally look for more ways to please God, and the cycle would progressively enlarge.

Jesus sent His apostles out in pairs of two (Mark 6:7), much like church visitations today. It gave them companionship, support, encouragement, appropriate witness, and protection. They would need it because not all the Israelites would be receptive to their sermons. Some would become downright belligerent.

The apostles were not prohibited from sharing their beliefs with Gentiles or Samaritans, but they were instructed to take their messages to the Jewish citizens first. Their first, apostolic mission was actually going to be a national survey to determine how many Israelites accepted Jesus as their Messiah. It didn't take long, because it didn't cover a very large area. At the most, Israel was only 75 miles wide by 125 miles long.

The apostles left with only the clothes on their backs. They took no food, supplies, or extra clothes. They were not allowed to charge anything for their ministry, but they were allowed to accept food and shelter from the people they helped. By limiting His apostles in this manner, Jesus taught them to trust Him for their basic needs.

Jesus taught the apostles to choose their host families carefully, because His integrity and their testimonies were at stake. He made it known that the most reputable host might not live in the largest house. The apostles were to assume the best of their hosts when they arrived and to bless the household with the greeting, "Peace to you." If the hosts did not extend their welcome, or if they rejected their messages, the apostles were instructed to shake the dust off their feet when they left that home or town (Matthew 10:14; Mark 6:11; Luke 9:5).

"Shaking off the dust" was a traditional, disdainful gesture faithful Jews often performed when they returned from Gentile areas. On their missions though, it signified that Jesus had been rejected and had rejected them in turn. It was a public testimony against them, and woe be to them on the day of judgement!

The apostles were very successful in healing the sick and casting out demons. As representatives of Jesus, they did everything in His name, so their healings demonstrated His power over the physical world. Their exorcisms demonstrated His power over the spiritual world. The apostles always considered their miracles to be secondary to their messages, but the crowds thought otherwise. They loved the miracles.

The displays of Jesus' extended power were unknown before the apostles began spreading it around their country. The people were amazed, and King Herod was becoming more and more alarmed. He had recently ordered the execution of John the Baptist for his righteous criticism against the royalty, and he was terrified that John had come back from the dead to haunt him. King Herod did not credit Jesus with deity but was convinced that He was a powerful prophet in line with Elijah and John the Baptist.

Jesus knew He was exposing His apostles to hatred and violence. He was sending them out like true prophets among false prophets, who would persecute them in attempts to destroy their missions. He told them, "I am sending you out like sheep among wolves" (Matthew 10:16). Nevertheless, Jesus expected them to keep their innocence and purity. They were not to be deterred by any controversy or hostility because ultimately, the unrighteous would fail!

# 19
## Feeding the Five Thousand

When the apostles returned to Jesus in Capernaum, they reported everything they had said and done on their mission. They were interrupted by huge crowds of people, though, when they realized Jesus had gathered them all together again.

Knowing His disciples needed privacy and rest, Jesus took them by boat to a remote area near Bethsaida, which was on the northern shore of Lake Galilee. The crowds followed them there on foot! Bethsaida was about four miles away by water and probably twice the distance by land, but some of the younger, faster ones actually got there before Him.

Jesus was not upset to see the crowds arrive. He felt sorry for them. He knew that the majority of followers were not really interested in His message. Most of them thought the kingdom of God was very interesting but didn't think repentance was really necessary for admittance. They had no interest in changing their daily lives, because they didn't know they were spiritually doomed.

Jesus thought of them as helpless victims, so He began teaching them many things. To Him they were like "sheep without a shepherd" (Mark 6:34). He knew that He wasn't capable of meeting their spiritual needs by Himself, but He cared about them all very deeply. So He kept preaching, hoping to turn some hearts.

Hours passed, and the disciples approached Jesus with their concerns. They said, "Send the people away so they can go to the surrounding countryside and villages, and buy themselves something to eat" (Mark 6:36). Jesus told His disciples to feed the people themselves. The disciples knew the impossibility. There were five thousand men, not counting the women and children (Matthew 14:21). They only had five sandwich rolls and two small fish.

Jesus took what little they brought to Him, looked up to heaven, gave thanks, broke the bread, and continually gave pieces to His disciples to distribute to the crowd. The multiplication of the small barley loaves apparently took place in His hands. He went through the same motion with the fish. They all ate and were all satisfied. The disciples picked up twelve small baskets of leftovers (Luke 9:12). Perhaps God also provided sustenance for the twelve who assisted in taking care of others.

After such a phenomenal miracle, the people began thinking that anyone who could do what Jesus had just done was surely be able to defeat the Romans and usher in a new era of Jewish rule. They circulated their thoughts: "Surely this is the Prophet who is to come into the world" (John 6:14). They were referring to what Moses had told the Israelites before he died: "The Lord your God will raise up for you a prophet like me from among your own brothers. You must listen to him" (Deuteronomy 18:15).

Supernaturally, Jesus knew that the well-intentioned but misguided followers in the crowds intended to make Him king by force. They wanted Him to exert His power and set up His kingdom immediately. He knew their political desires would jeopardize God's will, so He sent His disciples back toward Capernaum in their boat (Matthew 14:22) and then returned to dismiss the crowd before they became incited by mob mentality. Afterward, He withdrew (escaped) to the mountainside alone to pray. He knew He would be crucified within a year, but He still had much to expose, demonstrate, and endure.

During the fourth watch of the night (3 a.m. to 6 a.m.), Jesus *walked* out to join His disciples, who were still on the lake (Matthew 14:25; Mark 6:48; John 6:19). They were rowing against a strong wind, and the water was choppy. When they saw a figure walking toward them on the water, they thought it was a ghost! They didn't recognize Him, and once again, they were terrified. He calmed them by saying, "Take courage! It is I. Don't be afraid" (Matthew 14:27).

Peter replied, calling out, "Lord, if it's you … tell me to come to you on the water" (Matthew 14:28). Jesus complied and told him to come. So Peter bravely stepped out of the boat and actually started walking on the water toward Him. When the wind came up, though, Peter got frightened and started to sink. Jesus caught him and said, "You of little faith … why did you doubt?" (Matthew 14:31). Jesus had saved His disciples in the same boat once before, and they had seen more of His most awesome miracles than anyone else. They should have known they were always safe with Him and believed every word coming out of His mouth. The experience taught them that if they doubted their abilities under His coaching, they would lose them.

When Jesus and Peter climbed aboard, the wind instantly calmed down. Even though the disciples had not understood the significance of His miracle that afternoon (Mark 6:52), they knew at that precise moment in the boat that Jesus was truly the Son of God (Matthew 14:32). They didn't know what He planned to do, but they were thankful He had chosen them to assist Him in His mission.

When they rowed ashore at Gennesaret, just south of Capernaum, the residents recognized Jesus and quickly spread word of His arrival to the surrounding towns and villages. Throngs of people sought His healing miracles, so they brought everyone they knew who was sick to Him. They begged Him to let the sick people merely touch the edge of His cloak. He wouldn't even have to pronounce anything! Jesus complied, and all who touched Him were healed (Matthew 14:35, 36; Mark 6:54–56).

# 20
## Bread of Life

The next day, the crowd Jesus fed realized He and His disciples had left their remote area, so they left also and searched for Him. They went to Capernaum to see if He had returned to His headquarters. When they found Him, Jesus told them, "I tell you the truth, you are looking for me not because you saw miraculous signs, but because you ate the loaves and had your fill" (John 6:26).

Jesus knew many of His followers were very poor and very hungry. He fed them to comfort them, but He wanted them to become spiritually hungry. He wanted them to get beyond their hungry tummies and begin to focus on their hungry souls. He yearned for them to work for "food that endures to eternal life" instead of food that will perish (John 6:27).

The people didn't understand Jesus. They thought He was saying God required them to do some kind of good deeds to earn their way to heaven, and they wanted to know what they were. Jesus answered, "The work of God is this: to believe in the one He has sent" (John 6:29). God's only requirement to live with Him eternally is to believe Jesus is the Son of God. His kingdom is not about earning and deserving. It's all about believing and receiving!

"To believe in the one He has sent" ... Was Jesus referring to Himself as the Son of God? The people all knew He was a prophet of God and empowered by God, but the Son of God? If Jesus expected them to believe that, He would have to prove it to them with an extraordinary miracle. They knew Moses had given their ancestors bread from heaven to eat every day for forty years in the wilderness. If Jesus was who He claimed to be, He should be able to do the same thing, so they asked Him to send down manna from heaven.

Much to their surprise, Jesus offered something better. He agreed that God had indeed provided their ancestors with manna, but He explained that manna was a physical food that would perish, unlike the "true bread from heaven," which would not perish but provide eternal life to the entire world (John 6:32, 33). Naturally, that was the bread the crowd wanted. Bring it on! "Sir, from now on, give us this bread" (John 6:34). Forget the manna.

Their request opened the door for Jesus to finally proclaim His identity to the crowds: "I am the bread of life. He who comes to me will never go hungry, and he who believes in me will never go thirsty ... I have come down from heaven not to do my will, but to do the will of Him who sent me" (John 6:35–38).

This was the first of Jesus' seven great "I am" statements. It angered the majority of the crowd. They never expected Jesus to consider Himself to be equal with God! They knew that He came from Nazareth, which was right up the road. He wasn't supernatural; He was one of them! They quickly replied, "We know where this man is from; when the Christ comes, no one will know where He is from" (John 7:27).

Jesus' words were too hard for the crowd to swallow. Even the ones who followed Him devotedly to learn more about His kingdom were unable to get beyond their physical perspectives of Him. They weren't expecting a spiritual leader. They were expecting a powerful political Messiah. They shook their heads in dismay and murmured, "This is a hard teaching. Who can accept it?" (John 6:60). Even though Jesus displayed undeniable power and authority, the people started turning away from Him.

Jesus watched them walk away and knew He wouldn't be able to convince them of His identity before He was killed. His twelve disciples would be the ones to bring them back. He knew that most people followed Him out of curiosity, not out of belief. They always appeared when He entertained them, cured their illnesses, and supplied their needs. But they were not interested in His spiritual truths. He was getting annoyed by the thrill-seekers who came just to see His magic shows. He didn't want their applause. He wanted their commitment. But when He asked them for it, they balked. They were not looking for a king who spent His time telling stories. They were looking for a militant leader who spent his time raising an army that would defeat the Romans.

Jesus' popularity peaked with the feeding of the five thousand and plummeted after His sermon on the Bread of Life. Hostility began to spring from the people's unbelief, which hardened their hearts against Him. Many turned away. They "walked with Him no more" (John 6:66). They wanted His food and comforts, but they didn't want His requirements to follow Him. Sadly, their physical well-being was more important to them than the everlasting life He offered.

# 21
## Confrontation with the Pharisees

Seeing the crowds divide against Jesus and sensing a definite edge, the Pharisees and their scribes came from Jerusalem and gathered around Jesus. They hoped to gain more support from the multitudes by publicly criticizing His leadership. They asked Jesus, "Why do your disciples break the tradition of the elders? They don't wash their hands before they eat! (Matthew 15:2).

Jesus defended His disciples and turned the table on the Pharisees by asking, "Why do you break the command of God for the sake of your tradition?" (Matthew 15:3). His disciples had not observed the traditions of the elders, but since they had not broken any of God's written commandments, they were not unclean.

The traditions of the elders were something else Jesus opposed. They were rules that had been made up by Israeli leaders who had been exiled to Babylonia after Jerusalem was defeated in 586 BC. These infamous traditions existed in oral form only and were meant to bolster Jewish ceremonial laws. Over the following centuries, the traditions were increased and embellished. (Eventually, they were put into writing in the Mishna, but not until the end of the second century AD.) The authority of the traditions was not supported by Scripture, the true prophets, or by Jesus, but the Pharisees pompously considered them to be as binding as the Mosaic laws of the Old Testament.

The hand-washing tradition of the elders had nothing to do with cleaning dirty hands. It was a ceremonial tradition involving water that was poured on someone else's hands, whose fingers had to be pointing up. When the water dripped off at the wrist, more water was poured over the hands, this time with fingers pointing down. Finally, each hand was rubbed with the fist of the other hand.

Jesus considered such requirements needless and showy. He objected to the Pharisees, who ducked their responsibilities to God by supplanting Scripture with trivial traditions and then foolishly regarding them as the highest religious authority in Judaism. He accused the Pharisees of breaking the commandments of God by creating "wiggle room" with their traditions. "You have a fine way of setting aside the commands of God in order to observe your own traditions" (Mark 7:9).

Jesus proceeded to give them a blatant example of their unlawful practices. He reminded them that all Jews were supposed to honor their parents by assisting them financially if necessary. He rebuked them for creating a pious escape from this responsibility by declaring their assistance as corban, a gift to God. If a son became angry with his parents, he could declare his support money to them as corban and dedicate it to the temple instead, to be used for sacred purposes ... and hopefully helpful toward his own salvation.

Jesus condemned this heartless provision, because it allowed people to rationalize the neglect of their parents. He thought the Pharisees had become spiritual phonies, who were no longer genuinely religious or thoughtful of others. He called them "hypocrites," a term used to describe the original, professional actors on stage who wore masks, changing them each time they played different characters. Jesus saw the Pharisees as actors, wearing masks and playing religious roles for the multitudes to see. He told them they were the ones Isaiah referred to in Scripture when he spoke God's words, "These people honor me with their lips, but their hearts are far from me. They worship me in vain; their teachings are but rules taught by men" (Isaiah 29:13).

After this direct confrontation with the Pharisees and scribes, Jesus summoned the crowd and explained that there was a distinct difference between being ceremonially unclean and morally unclean. "Nothing outside a man can make him 'unclean' by going into him. Rather, it is what comes out of a man that makes him 'unclean'" (Mark 7:15).

Peter privately asked Jesus to further explain this comparison for him and the rest of the disciples. Jesus told them very simply that food cannot make a person unclean, because it doesn't go into the heart. It goes into the stomach and is later eliminated. Words, though, can definitely make a person unclean, because they come from the heart and are voiced through the mouth. Words that are mean, vulgar, untruthful, or contrary to the laws of God will instantly make a person unclean. The Pharisees had defiled themselves with their false doctrines. The disciples had not.

The Pharisees were furious because Jesus had humiliated them in public—again. He had pushed the conflicts between them to a breaking point. He wasn't going to honor their traditions, and they were not going to honor Him. They were determined to eliminate Him before He completely ruined the control and the lifestyle they had established over the years for themselves.

When the disciples told Jesus He had ruffled the Pharisees' feathers, He told them not to worry about their offended pride, because God the Father was going to uproot every religious system He didn't plant (Matthew 15:13). The Pharisees and all their followers were doomed. They were blind guides leading blind people, and they were all going to fall into the pit (Matthew 15:14).

Sadly, the Jews in ancient history had been led astray by their religious leaders. God sent Jesus to lead them back to Him. Some would accept Jesus as their Savior and follow Him. Most, though, would not.

## 22
## Outlying Areas

The chasm between ceremonial traditions and true religious spirituality continued to grow deeper and wider. Jesus knew His mission in Galilee was finished, and He withdrew from Israel. He wanted to evade further conflicts with His opponents, so they wouldn't attempt to kill Him before He was ready. He also wanted to devote more time alone with His disciples. He took them into the outlying Gentile areas. It was time to disclose His true identity and His full mission to His disciples. They needed to know who He was and exactly what He was going to do.

First, Jesus took them about forty miles northwest to the Mediterranean coast. Then to avoid Galilee, He led them due east and south to the ten cities of the Decapolis. Finally, they went north to Caesarea-Philippi, before heading to the cross in Jerusalem. He was following the will, the plan, and very specific details of God the Father.

On the Mediterranean coast, Jesus introduced His disciples to the Phoenician cities of Tyre and Sidon, in what is today's Lebanon. When they entered Tyre, a Greek woman begged Jesus to drive a demon from her daughter. She actually interrupted Him as He was teaching His disciples about their future ministries.

Jesus wasn't looking for a public ministry among Gentiles, so He refused her initial request. But she was not to be deterred (Mark 7:28)! Her faith in Him was strong. She called Him "Lord" and continued her pleas. Jesus rewarded her faith in Him and her persistence by casting out her daughter's demon. When she went home, her child was lying on the bed, and the demon was gone (Mark 7:30).

From Tyre, Jesus led His disciples twenty miles north to the city of Sidon and then east across the Jordan River. From there they moved south, along the eastern shore of Lake Galilee. They entered the region of the Decapolis, a Gentile stronghold of Greek customs and beliefs.

His reputation preceded Him. The people there were not Jewish, but they knew all about Jesus of Nazareth and His supernatural miracles. They brought a man to Him who was deaf and could hardly talk. They begged Jesus to place His hands on the man. Jesus took the blind man aside to open his ears and loosen his tongue. The man began to speak clearly (Mark 7:35).

Jesus told the people not to broadcast His miracle. He didn't want more publicity, which would divert His final instructions and revelations to His disciples. He didn't mind helping Gentiles as their needs arose, but He had no intention to preach to the masses again, as He had in Galilee. He wanted to focus on His chosen Twelve, because they would be the ones who would keep His ministry alive after His crucifixion during the coming Passover.

The Gentiles did not honor His request. They were overwhelmed with amazement and told everyone who would listen about the man He cured in the Decapolis. Consequently, great crowds arrived, and they brought a huge number of handicapped people with them. They laid them at Jesus' feet, and He healed them all. Furthermore, unlike today's faith healers, Jesus didn't charge anything for His services. The Gentiles stayed there with Him for three days on empty stomachs. They were eager to learn about His kingdom, and watch Him heal their friends. They continually praised the awesome God of Israel (Matthew 15:31).

Jesus felt sorry for this hungry crowd of about four thousand men, plus women and children. He knew they would collapse if He sent them away without eating, so He called His disciples together to tell them He wanted to feed the crowd. Slow-wittedly, His disciples asked Him, "Where in this remote place can anyone get enough bread to feed them?" (Mark 8:1). Had they already forgotten about feeding a larger crowd a few days earlier? They exhibited an unbelievable lack of understanding. They had a long way to go in spiritual perception!

Very patiently, Jesus gathered their seven loaves of bread, gave thanks, broke them into pieces, and gave them to His disciples to distribute to the multitude. He sent the crowd away after the disciples collected the leftovers in large baskets. Then Jesus got into a boat with His disciples and rowed across Lake Galilee to the western shore (Matthew 15:39).

When the Pharisees and Sadducees heard that Jesus was back in their vicinity, they went to test Him. They asked Him for further proof of His messianic claims. They wanted an astronomical miracle, also. Jesus sighed. His countless number of miracles on earth should have been more than enough to convince them of His deity, but He answered them, saying, "A wicked and adulterous generation looks for a miraculous sign, but none will be given it except for the sign of Jonah" (Matthew 16:4). Then with a note of finality, Jesus walked away.

The adultery to which Jesus referred was a spiritual adultery, an unfaithfulness to God. He refused to accommodate their spiritual blindness. They wanted a sign from heaven, but He gave them a sign from Scripture. Just as Jonah had spent three days in the belly of a large fish, Jesus was going to spend three days in the heart of the earth (Matthew 12:40).

The Pharisees knew exactly what Jesus was implying about Jonah, because they were experts of Scripture. The disciples would understand His comparison in less than a year, because the ultimate sign that would verify His claims of being the Son of God and the long-awaited Messiah would be his resurrection.

Jesus left the religious leaders abruptly. He got in the boat and headed for the northern shore of Lake Galilee. Once under way, He warned the disciples to "be on guard against the yeast of the Pharisees and Sadducees" (Matthew 16:6). His disciples missed His spiritual point again. They thought He was talking about the bread they had forgotten to pack for their journey. Jesus rebuked them for their disconnected thoughts. "You of little faith ... How is it you don't understand that I was not talking to you about bread?" (Matthew 16:9, 11). The disciples then realized the yeast (leaven) referred to the teachings of the Pharisees and Sadducees. Jesus wouldn't have warned them about something good. He was warning them against something evil—the false doctrines and sinister influence of their religious leaders. Jesus wanted them to mind the gap, or know the difference between what He said and did, versus what the Pharisees said and did.

After disembarking, Jesus led His disciples way north to the region of Caesarea-Philippi, which was under the rule of Herod's brother, Philip. There, He asked the disciples who they thought He was. They replied some people thought He was John the Baptist, Elijah, Jeremiah the weeping prophet, or one of the other true prophets. They had not answered Jesus' specific question, though, so He asked again, "But what about you? ... Who do you say I am?" (Matthew 16:15; Mark 8:28; Luke 9:20).

Simon Peter answered as spokesman for all of them: "You are the Christ, the Son of the living God" (Matthew 16:16).

"Christ" is a title that means the "Anointed One." The Hebrew equivalent of Christ is Messiah. Prophets, priests, and kings in the Old Testament were all anointed with oil, which symbolized a consecration (a setting aside) for ministry by God (1 Kings 19:16; Leviticus 4:5, 16; 1 Samuel 24:6, 10). When Peter claimed that Jesus Christ was the Anointed One, he claimed He was the ultimate prophet, priest, and King (Isaiah 61:1). He claimed that Jesus was the Messiah!

Jesus blessed Peter for his confession of personal faith and told him his revelation had not come from man but from His Father in heaven (Matthew 16:17). Peter had not learned His true identity from Jesus or anyone else. Peter's eyes and heart had been opened by God the Father through the Holy Spirit.

Jesus was thankful that all His disciples now knew the truth, but He asked them to keep it to themselves for a little while longer. He had more to teach them before they broadcast their new revelations. They now knew who He was, but they still did not know exactly what He came to do. Their assumptions of His full mission were wrong. He was not the conquering hero they expected their Messiah to be. He had not come to save them from the Romans. He had come to save them and the rest of the world, from going to hell, because their many sins had separated them from God.

Jesus knew He only had about six more months to be with His disciples. He would use His little time remaining to prepare them for His death, resurrection, and ascension.

# 23
## Turning Point

Caesarea-Philippi was a turning point. Once His disciples knew He was the Son of Man and the Son of God, Jesus resolutely set out for the cross. He was well aware of His fate, and He faced it willingly (Mark 8:31; 9:30, 31). He came to earth to give His life as a payment for all sins, which had created a barrier between God and humanity. He knew His supreme sacrifice would be the only way for people to reestablish the right relationship with God. He now needed to explain the rest of His full mission to His disciples, and He knew they wouldn't like it. He told them He, "must go to Jerusalem and suffer many things at the hands of the elders, chief priests, and teachers of the law ... and that He must be killed, and on the third day, be raised to life" (Matthew 16:21).

Peter was the first to object. He quietly took Jesus aside and complained, "Never, Lord ... this shall never happen to you!" (Matthew 16:22).

Jesus rebuked Peter: "Get behind me, Satan! You are a stumbling block to me; you do not have in mind the things of God, but the things of men" (Matthew 16:23).

Poor foot-in-mouth-Peter! He had no intentions of thwarting Jesus' mission or being a spokesperson for Satan. He just wanted Jesus to avoid pain. Peter would learn many more details in the remaining six months with Jesus, but his characteristic impulsiveness certainly started him off on the wrong sandal.

Jesus turned back to the rest of His bewildered disciples and assured them no matter what happened to Him, God the Father would reward all of them accordingly, for denying themselves and following His only Son. Jesus also promised some of them would see Him coming into His kingdom before they died (Matthew 16:24–28; Mark 8:34; 9:1; Luke 9:23–27). Little did they know how fast that last promise would be fulfilled!

A week or so later, Jesus went up on a mountainside to pray and invited Peter, James, and John to join Him. These three were often seen alone with Jesus (Matthew 26:37; Mark 5:37; 13:3). Scripture does not explain why they were allowed to witness things other disciples were not, but the three fishermen definitely comprised an inner circle of Jesus' friends. None of them were easy to instruct. All were impulsive. James and John were known as "Sons of Thunder" for wanting to call fire down from heaven to destroy unbelievers (Mark 3:17; Luke 9:54). Perhaps those three disciples needed the most convincing.

As Jesus prayed, He was completely transfigured before Peter, James, and John. ". . .the appearance of his face changed, and his clothes became as bright as a flash of lightning" (Luke 9:29). This dazzling light of glory did not spotlight Him. It actually shone from within! It showcased the greatest hope of all Christians—that we will all be translated ourselves when Jesus comes again, and that we will all gain perfect bodies when we meet Him in midair during the Rapture. The Old Testament saints who have died will be raised first. Then those of us who are alive will be instantly changed (1 Corinthians 15:51).

The three stunned disciples also saw two men appear with Jesus in their glorious splendor. One was Moses, who was present as the representative of the Old Testament law. The other one was Elijah, who was present as the representative of the Old Testament prophets. Both had foretold of Jesus' death, and they were there on the mountain to discuss it with Him in detail.

Peter, James, and John were spellbound and did not know what to say. Peter blurted out some pious words of little context without knowing what he was saying. Typical, blundering Peter! He was interrupted by a cloud, which enveloped them. A voice coming from the cloud said, "This is my Son, whom I love; with him I am well pleased. Listen to him!" (Matthew 17:5).

The disciples were terrified by seeing Jesus' glorification and hearing the voice of God. It was all too much. Their minds grew fuzzy, their eyelids became heavy, and they fell to the ground face-first. The spiritual world will always be too much for mortals.

Jesus was right there to comfort them. He told them not to be afraid—and to get up. When they rose to their feet, they were alone with Jesus in His normal countenance. (Years later, Peter wrote about their surreal experience of witnessing a miniature version of the coming kingdom. See 2 Peter 1: 16-18.)

As they were leaving the holy mountain, Jesus told them not to tell anyone what they had seen until the Son of Man had been raised from the dead (Mark 9:9). His request confused the disciples, because the scribes had taught them Elijah would return preceding the coming of the Lord. Had they missed it? They knew very little about prophecy, so they asked Jesus about Elijah.

Jesus told them that they were partially right. Four hundred years earlier, Malachi did predict Elijah's return, but his prophecy had already been fulfilled. Elijah had already come again and gone. The Jewish leaders had failed to accept him, though, as someone sent by God. Furthermore, they didn't like what he was saying, so they had him killed. Without skipping a beat, Jesus informed them the same thing was about to happen to <u>Him</u>. The religious leaders did not accept Him as their Messiah, nor did they like what He was saying, so they were plotting His death.

The disciples realized instantly that Jesus had been referring to John the Baptist (Matthew 17:13), but they were perplexed once again. Didn't John deny that he was Elijah before he was beheaded? Yes, but the people still knew Elijah never died *physically*. He had been whisked away by a chariot of fire (2 Kings 2:11). Some of them thought Elijah had reappeared in the form of John the Baptist, but when they confronted him about it, John denied their suspicions.

John the Baptist knew who he was. He was definitely a prophet, but he had not returned to earth from a former life. As predicted by an angel of the Lord before he had been born (Luke 1:14–17), and also predicted earlier in Galilee by Jesus (Matthew 11:12, 14), John had come to earth in the spirit and power of Elijah but not in the physical form of the great prophet. Therefore, John truthfully announced that he was simply a voice in the wilderness, calling, "Make straight the way for the Lord" (John 1:19–23).

When Jesus, Peter, James, and John returned to the other disciples, a man asked Jesus to have mercy on his son, whose seizures were causing him to fall into fire and water. Sadly, the disciples had tried but failed to cure the boy. Jesus criticized His disciples for their weak faith and healed the boy by driving the demon out of him.

The disciples asked Jesus in private why they had been able to drive out demons before, when Jesus had commissioned them as His apostles, but not this time for the boy, when Jesus had simply been out of the area. Jesus said, "Because you have so little faith" (Matthew 17:20). The disciples had God's power but didn't use it. They relied on their own confidence and "gifts" but should have relied on God's power and given the glory to Him.

When they returned to Galilee, Jesus told them again of His death and resurrection. He never mentioned one without the other. He said, "The Son of Man is going to be betrayed into the hands of men. They will kill him, and on the third day, he will be raised to life" (Matthew 17:22,23).

The disciples were filled with grief. They didn't understand His resurrection, but they knew He was the One who would shoulder their sins and intercede with God on their behalf (Isaiah 53:12). They knew Jesus was the Son of God and the Jewish Messiah, so why was He talking about His death? It was absolutely unthinkable! It didn't fit into their program at all. He wasn't supposed to die. He was supposed to come in glory and rule the world forever. Worldwide Jewish rule. Hallelujah! Little did they know then that Jesus would come to earth twice—first as a humble servant, and second in power and glory.

By the time they reached Capernaum, the disciples had developed new ideas about Jesus being buried and rising again. Maybe He would introduce His kingdom when He rose again. Maybe that would be when the world would recognize His power. Would His twelve disciples have important positions then? Surely they would sit near the throne of God. Who would sit the closest? What would be the protocol? They started to bicker among themselves and jockey for key positions of status. Finally, they asked Him outright, "Who is the greatest in the kingdom of heaven?" (Matthew 18:1).

Jesus knew their thoughts and understood their foolish human nature. He responded patiently. He called a child who was playing nearby and asked him to stand in their midst. Jesus faced His disciples and taught them His message with simple imagery. "Unless you change and become like children, you will never enter the kingdom of heaven. Therefore, whoever humbles himself like this child, is the greatest in the kingdom of heaven" (Matthew 18:3, 4).

Jesus defined conversion by the phrase, "become like children." He wasn't talking about going backward into a former childhood. He was encouraging them to take small steps forward into a new, spiritual life of joy. Humble themselves. Confess their sins. Repent. Ask for forgiveness. Ask God to help them learn His will and walk in His ways.

Children have no resources of their own, so they have nothing to offer God to garner His attention or earn His praise. Their faith is pure because it's a simple one. It's nothing more than a trusting dependence on God Almighty. That's what Jesus asked of His followers. That's all God wants from us. God loves us because of who He is, not because of anything we have or do! It's a love that far surpasses all understanding. "Trust in the Lord with all your heart, and lean not upon your own understanding" (Proverbs 3:5). His ways and thoughts are higher than ours (Isaiah 55:9).

Jesus' key word was "change." Unless His disciples submitted their proud selves to Him and started spiritually anew (born again) as children of faith, they wouldn't get into the kingdom of heaven. Jesus emphasized entrance. Rank or position of the believers was not important. The childlikeness of believers is what's important.

Jesus left His headquarters in Capernaum and never returned. He kept traveling south through Samaria, the Transjordan regions, and Judea. He sent messengers ahead of Him to make travel arrangements. But the Samaritans did not offer Him any lodgings this time, because He was heading toward Jerusalem, not away from it as before. They wanted nothing to do with anyone who mingled with Judeans.

Remember, the Samaritans were descendants of Jews who had married Gentiles after Israel was defeated by Babylon in 586

BC. They developed their own pagan, religious rites, which they continued to practice on Mt. Gerizim, even after the pious Jews returned to Jerusalem from exile in Babylon to rebuild their city and their beloved temple. The five hundred–year rift between the mixed Samaritans and the pure Jews continued to widen, but Jesus always ministered to both groups. He considered them all to be lost sheep, but the Samaritans had definitely wandered further away from the orthodox flock.

James and his brother, John, were furious that the Samaritans wouldn't welcome Jesus as they had before. That is when the two disciples asked Him if He wanted them to call down fire from heaven to destroy the inhospitable Samaritans (Luke 9:54), like the prophet Elijah had done centuries earlier (2 Kings 1:10–12).

Jesus gently rebuked James and John, and later referred to them as "Sons of Thunder" (Mark 3:17). He wanted them to exemplify grace—not retaliation—as His followers. Anger was not the way to handle opposition (Luke 9:55). Jesus had come to earth to save not to destroy … to sow not to reap … to teach not to judge. Judgment lay in other hands for other times.

To help His disciples and His followers understand the humble world He wanted them to enter, Jesus used parables to describe the kingdom of heaven in greater detail and to simplify its meaning. He asked them to live their lives like servants who had been put in charge of a man's (a master's) property before he left on a long trip. The man gave them assigned tasks and told the one at the door to watch for his return (Mark 13:34). The man also asked them to "be dressed ready for service, and keep your lamps burning like men waiting for their master to return from a wedding banquet, so that when he comes and knocks, they can immediately open the door for him" (Luke 12:35). Believers were always to follow the Master's orders, and be prepared for His return. Those who followed His orders would be rewarded. Those who didn't would be punished.

Using another parable, Jesus told the story of a man going on a long journey who called his servants and entrusted his property to them before he left. He gave five talents of money to one servant, two talents to the second servant, and one talent to a third servant. A talent was an enormous amount of money in the first century. It was worth about two years of servants' wages. The three chosen servants were to spend their master's money according to their individual abilities and put it to work for him (Matthew 25:14).

Jesus always tied responsible stewardship of resources (money, time, ability, and spiritual gifts) to the coming kingdom of God. Believers were always supposed to invest their gifts and opportunities in ways that served God and, thereby, advanced His kingdom. Those who lived their lives to please God and help others would be blessed for their humble service on His return. Those who squandered their opportunities by living to please themselves would be disciplined.

In a world driven by self-interest, Jesus wanted the people to gain an opportunity to live for a higher purpose than the trivial pursuit of earthly comforts and achievements. He wanted them to care more about the hereafter than the here and now, so He emphasized the importance of spiritual development over the acquisition of material possessions (Luke 12:22-34).

The problem within the multitudes, though, was their intention to play today and repent tomorrow. Most of them assumed they had ample time in this world to prepare for the next. Therefore, they had little incentive to abandon their current activities and sign up for a radical new game plan of reversed values. "Me first" seemed to be working just fine for them! They saw nothing wrong with their efforts to keep God happy by obeying a few of His commandments. But they had no intentions to change their daily lives.

Jesus disagreed with their assumptions. He assured them that calamities come suddenly and unexpectedly, and there is a definite correlation between catastrophes and depravities (Luke 13:1–5). Humans will always be subject to destruction, because normal human behavior is selfish. No one, however, is guaranteed time to prepare for death. Jesus called them to confess their sins and failures immediately, and to ask God for His forgiveness before it was too late.

To simplify His bold statements, Jesus told a story about a planter, who was going to cut down his fig tree unless it started to produce figs (Luke 13:6–9). Just as the planter was not going to wait forever for his fig tree to produce fruit, neither is God going to wait forever for people to start walking in His ways.

People still living were fortunate, but they needed to seek the LORD while He could still be found and call upon Him while He was still near (Isaiah 55:6). They could still change the focus of their lives before the gavel fell. They still had a choice to repent or live without the many blessings of God. Jesus hoped they make the right choice.

God does not force His will on anyone; He champions free will. He always has. He always will. If someone asks Him to change their will or desires, though, that's a different story. God knows hearts, so if anyone comes to Him humbly, with genuine desires to turn from what's wrong and toward what's right, He will help them by changing them from the inside out.

Only God can do that. People cannot change human nature. Many people lead miserable lives as addicts, criminals, or misfits. They cannot permanently walk away from temptations, addictive needs, or deviant lifestyles by themselves. Try as they might, they eventually slip back into former patterns and weaknesses.

What can they do? They can change teams. They can sincerely ask for God's help. They can ask Him to enter their lives and lead them on His paths.

God knows earnest souls and rewards humble requests! He is near everyone who calls on Him in truth (Psalm 145:18). He will intervene for those who submit themselves to Him. He will lead them through the Holy Spirit and free them from their earthly shackles. Best of all, He will replace their anxieties with His peace. Only then will they be able to persevere on their higher roads of choice, because the power behind them will always be greater than the tasks ahead of them. "Greater is He who is in me than he who is in the world" (1 John 4:4).

A few people heard Jesus and stepped out of the crowds to repent and follow Him. He welcomed them, but warned them before they made their final commitment that life with Him would not always be comfortable or easy. He told them,

(1) He no longer had headquarters or lodging. "The Son of Man has nowhere to lay His head" (Luke 9:58).

(2) His call to discipleship had no margin for detours, distractions, or family precedence. They wouldn't be able to wait for funerals. "Let the dead bury their own" (Luke 9:60).

(3) Once they committed their lives to Him, they wouldn't be able to go back to their former ways. "No one having put his hand to the plow and looking back, is fit for the kingdom of God" (Luke 9:62).

The people understood. They knew how difficult it was for Lot's wife to leave her home in Sodom. When she looked back, she was turned into a pillar of salt (Genesis 19:26).

Jesus left the crowds with His disciples to discuss a short trip they would be taking to Jerusalem for the Feast of Tabernacles. Attendance was mandatory for faithful adult males, and He would be there, though He was not going for the first days of the celebration. Jesus knew the authorities would be watching for Him. He did not want to turn the weeklong festival into an open conflict with religious leaders, so He sent His disciples there a few days ahead of Him.

## 24
## Feast of Tabernacles

When Jesus arrived in Jerusalem, He entered the temple quietly and then started teaching Scripture in the open courts, just like the rabbis did.

The people knew that Jesus had never studied at any of the great rabbinical centers, so they were always amazed by His profound mastery of Scripture. Jesus told them that His words came directly from God: "My teaching is not my own. It comes from Him who sent me" (John 7:16). Jesus didn't learn Scripture from man, like the rabbis did, who relied on the authority of others. Jesus was His own authority. (Matthew 7:28, 29). His knowledge was God-given and supernatural.

A few people in the Jerusalem crowds believed Jesus and hung on every word He said. They thought He was truthful and thoroughly good. Others had been negatively influenced by the religious leaders, and they remained skeptical of Him. They thought He was a con artist and attributed His vast knowledge to demon possession (John 7:20).

Public opinions of Jesus throughout Israel were very diverse, because perceptions of Him varied greatly. People who traveled to Jerusalem from the rural areas of other provinces knew nothing about the religious leaders' opposition of Jesus, or their plans to kill Him for breaking their Sabbath laws or making Himself equal with God (John 5:18). The people from Judea were better informed about the conflicts, but they were divided among themselves because of their personal differences in knowledge of Scripture. Some of them were surprised Jesus continued to boldly claim His divinity in spite of the threats from the religious authorities. They asked each other, "Isn't this the man they are trying to kill? Here He is speaking publicly, and they are not saying a word to him" (John 7:25, 26). Others wondered if the religious leaders knew that Jesus really was the Messiah and had wisely decided not to mess with the Son of God. They vacillated, because most of them expected their Messiah to appear suddenly out of nowhere. But Jesus had not done that. Everyone knew He was from Nazareth, so He couldn't be the Messiah, could He?

Knowing their thoughts, Jesus was well aware people knew Him in an earthly sense but not in a spiritual one. They didn't know God, either, so He called out to the crowds in the temple courtyard and said, "Yes, you know me, and you know where I'm from … but you do not know Him" (John 7:28).

Their rejections of Jesus revealed their spiritual anemia. They didn't have the Son, so they didn't have the Father, either (1 John 2:23).

Jesus' statement was a supreme insult to the religious leaders who thought of themselves as spiritually keen and acutely perceptive. Of course they knew God. How dare a carpenter from Nazareth accuse them of being spiritually lean. They were enraged. It was one thing to reject their traditional laws. It was quite another to be repeatedly roasted in public.

Their anger didn't faze Jesus. His verbal assault only continued to escalate. Next, He proclaimed, "I know him because I am from him, and he sent me" (John 7:29).

The leaders regarded Jesus' claim of divine origin as blasphemous and tried to seize Him. But no one was able to lay a hand on Him. His evasion was supernatural. God's timetable and plans for Him would not allow Him to be captured. "His time had not yet come" (John 7:30).

Even after the frenzied failure to capture Jesus, a small remnant in the crowd still had faith that Jesus was exactly who He claimed to be. They knew the religious leaders would not have reacted to Him with such hatred if Jesus were just another religious fake. Jesus was obviously a serious threat to their rule and leadership. To convince the naysayers of His deity, these loyal believers bravely asked, "When the Christ comes, will He do more miraculous signs than this man?" (John 7:31).

The Pharisees and chief priests lost all composure as they listened to the crowd's approval of Jesus, and they sent the temple guards to arrest Him. These guards were Levites, who had been religiously trained. They were in charge of maintaining order in the temple. They operated as a type of police force to subdue any skirmishes in or near the temple.

It was unusual for the Pharisees and the chief priests to work together. They were political and religious opponents. Most of the chief priests were Sadducees, who didn't believe the dire warnings of the true prophets. They didn't believe in angels, demons, or resurrection. They favored the wealthy Jews, not the common multitudes, but they joined the Pharisees in their mutual hatred of Jesus, who opposed both parties.

The temple guards didn't have to look far to find Jesus. He was still preaching in the temple courts during the last days of the Feast of Tabernacles. When they found Him, He was telling His listeners, "I am with you for only a short time, and then I go to the one who sent me. You will look for me, but you will not find me; and where I am, you cannot come" (John 7:33). The religious leaders who were listening were puzzled, but the temple guards were intrigued. So they hung around to hear more.

Jesus was referring to His return to heaven and reunion with His Father, which would happen after the religious leaders had Him killed. But His spiritual explanation went right over most heads. All the leaders could do was mock Jesus for what they considered to be very bizarre statements.

During most Tabernacles, Jesus kept a low profile. He came to teach during the middle of the week. He came alone and didn't walk into the temple through any of the main gates. On the last day of the festival, though, He made two dramatic appearances at crucial moments to reveal His true identity to everyone and to invite them to accept Him as their Messiah. He used the two major themes of Tabernacles, water and light, as object lessons and opportunities to present Himself as the source of eternal life.

The Feast of Tabernacles was a joyous one and the most popular of the three primary Jewish festivals—Passover, Pentecost, and Tabernacles. It was known for its water-drawing and lamp-lighting rites, which commemorated the water and "pillar of light" God provided for the Israelites during their forty-year exodus from Egyptian slavery. After the torches (lamps) were lighted, the people celebrated by dancing through the evening while holding burning torches and singing songs of praise to God.

In the few centuries before Christ was born, a new tradition was introduced during tabernacles. The high priest would fill a gold pitcher with water from the Pool of Siloam and carry it back to the temple in a grand procession. The people followed, waving palm branches. When they entered the inner temple court, three trumpet blasts sounded to mark the joy of the occasion. The people quoted the prophet Isaiah: "With joy you will draw water from the wells of salvation" (Isaiah 12:3). The priest marched around the altar while the temple choir sang the Hallel (the praises in Psalms 113–118). The priest poured the water on the altar during the morning sacrifice to God. On the last day of Tabernacles, the ceremony was extended. The priest marched around the altar seven times before pouring out the water. This was done in memory of the seven circuits made around the city of Jericho before the walls came tumbling down.

Jesus used this last pouring ritual to make a very bold announcement: "If anyone is thirsty, let him come to me and drink. Whoever believes in me, as the Scripture has said, streams of living water will flow from within him" (John 7:37,38). Jesus was revealing Himself to the multitudes as the One who would provide the living water that gives eternal life to humankind, just as He had revealed Himself to the Samaritan woman at Jacob's well (John 4:14) and to Nicodemus (John 3:5).

Jesus was referring to the Holy Spirit, who would come to believers after His death, resurrection, and ascension (John 7:39). Believers will be satisfied themselves, and they will also become a river to satisfy others.

After this last water-pouring ritual, the temple guards returned empty-handed to the Pharisees and the chief priests. They had not arrested Jesus. When asked why they didn't follow orders, the guards responded, "No one ever spoke the way this man does" (John 7:46). The temple guards obviously had been very moved by Jesus' sound character and powerful teaching. His words recalled Isaiah's invitation to come to the water: "Come, all you who are thirsty, come to the water ... come, buy ... without money and without cost" (Isaiah 55:1).

Jesus' three words—"thirsty," "come," "drink"—actually summarize the gospel invitation still offered today: (1) recognize your need, (2) come to the providing Source, and (3) receive what you need. Thirsty, needy souls should crave to come to Lord Jesus and drink (receive) the salvation He offers.

The Pharisees were miffed by the guards' response. It was wrenching for them to see people siding with Jesus when they themselves were so vehemently opposed to Him. In exasperation, they asked the crowd, "Has any of the rulers, or of the Pharisees believed in Him? No!" (John 7:48,49a). They accused the temple guards of being deceived and considered all the believers to be ignorant of the Jewish law and consequently subject to God's curses (John 7:49b). Ironically, the curses worked the other way! God's wrath fell upon the arrogant Pharisees for rejecting His Son. (John 3:36). The rulers were condemning themselves by their continual opposition to Jesus.

Nicodemus, a Pharisee and notable religious authority, had not made up his mind about the claims of Jesus, but he sensed a mistake in the procedures against Jesus. He didn't defend Jesus directly, but he raised a legal concern in His favor: "Does our law condemn anyone without first hearing him to find out what he is doing?" (John 7:51). Nicodemus had made an accurate plea for justice, but the Pharisees rejected it and mocked him as well as Jesus. They replied, "Are you from Galilee, too? Look into it, and you will find that a prophet does not come out of Galilee" (John 7:52). They were wrong. Jonah came from Galilee!

Jesus spoke to the crowd at Tabernacles again during the lamp-lighting ceremony. On the last day of the festival, the people commemorate God's "pillars of light" for their protection and guidance during the exodus with a torch parade and the lighting of huge candelabras in the temple. Jesus used that final event to make another profound analogy. He declared, "I am the light of the world.

Whoever follows me will not walk in darkness, but will have the light of life" (John 8:12).

This was His second of seven "I am" statements. He was claiming to be God, but the rulers missed His connections at that moment. The light was shining in the darkness, but the darkness didn't understand it (John 1:5). Some people can have all the lights on and still remain in the dark.

Jesus had announced that He was the fulfillment of prophetic Scripture. He revealed His true identity to everyone present. He had claimed to be the One who will bring light and living water to those who believe in Him (Zecharia 14:7, 8). He had claimed to be the One who will be a light for His people (Isaiah 60:19–22), as well as a light for the whole earth (Isaiah 42:6; 49:6).

The Pharisees challenged His claims immediately. Jesus accepted their challenges and proceeded to condemn them in public. In doing so, He turned their smoldering dislike for Him into an intense hatred.

The ensuing verbal showdown went something like this.

Jesus:      I am the light of the world (John 8:12).
Pharisees:  You cannot prove it if you are the only one testifying to us. You need a witness (John 8:13).
Jesus:      I am not alone. I am standing here with my Father, who sent me (John 8:16, 18).
Pharisees:  Where is your Father? (John 8:19a).
Jesus:      You do not know my Father. You do not know me, and you don't know God (John 8:19b).
Jesus:      If you don't believe that I am who I say I am, then you will die in your sin (John 8:24).
Pharisees:  Who are you? (John 8:25).
Jesus:      I am the One I claim to be, and I am not alone. The One who sent me is with me (John 8:28, 29).
Jesus:      My truth will set you free (John 8:32).
Pharisees:  We don't need to be set free. We have never been slaves (John 8:33).

| | |
|---|---|
| Jesus: | Yes you have been! You are the slaves of sin and you need a Savior to forgive you (John 8:34). |
| Pharisees: | No we don't! We are the children of Abraham, and our heritage guarantees us a place in heaven (John 8:39a). |
| Jesus: | Physically, you came from Abraham, but spiritually there is no resemblance. If you were Abraham's children, you would do good things, like he did (John 8:39b). |
| Pharisees: | We are not illegitimate like you are. (The gossips of their day alleged that Jesus had been born out of wedlock.) God is our only Father (John 8:41). |
| Jesus: | Your father is the devil, who is a murderer and a liar (John 8:44). |
| Pharisees: | You're nothing but a demon-possessed Samaritan (John 8:48). |
| Jesus: | No I'm not. But I honor my Father, I tell the truth, and I have power over death (John 8:49–51). |
| Pharisees: | Do you think you are greater than our father, Abraham? Just who do you think you are? (John 8:53). |
| Jesus: | Your father, Abraham, looked for the One who would fulfill everything that God promised and rejoiced at the mere thought of seeing My day (John 8:56). |
| Pharisees: | You claim to have seen Abraham, and you aren't even fifty years old (John 8:57). |
| Jesus: | I tell you the truth. Before Abraham was born, I am. (John 8:58). |

Jesus wasn't just claiming that He lived before Abraham. Jesus was claiming eternal existence. He was claiming to be God! "I am" was God's designation of Himself (Exodus 3:14).

The Pharisees understood His claim implicitly this time, but they didn't believe Him. On the contrary, most of them thought that

His claims were irreverent, so they picked up stones to kill Him for blasphemy, as their Scripture dictated (Leviticus 24:16).

Was it still legal in the first century for the Jews to stone anyone to death? No! When the Romans took over Judea and began to rule it through a Roman procurator in AD 6, the right to execute anyone was taken away from the Jews and given to the Roman governor in Judea. (Pontius Pilate was the governor of Judea during Jesus' ministry.) Nevertheless, the religious leaders were incensed over Jesus' preposterous statements, so they attempted a frenzied mob action in lieu of legal proceedings.

Their efforts failed, because Jesus made another miraculous escape. He hid Himself and then quietly slipped away from the bloodhounds of hate (John 8:59). His hour had not yet come.

Why didn't the majority of Pharisees believe Jesus' claims? Because they couldn't. They had completely sold out to power and riches. Jesus' compassion for others was very nice, but the Pharisees didn't think they had to adopt all His attributes. Their eyes were blinded, their ears were blocked, and their hearts were hardened by their prejudice, corruption, and disbelief.

Jesus had placed the Pharisees on the spot by revealing His true identity. They now had to accept or reject Him. He was either God and Savior, or He wasn't.

Most Pharisees rejected Jesus. Life was very good for them under Roman rule, and Jesus simply did not fit into their game plan. They were into physical pleasures, not spiritual ones, so they had no need for spiritual leadership. They were doing just fine without a Savior in their midst. And if He would just go away, they would do even better.

This showdown with the Pharisees made Jesus the talk of all nearby towns. He became the "breaking news" in homes, markets, taverns, and synagogues. His rise in popularity enraged religious leaders. They became more determined to expose His next miracle as a fraud, because they knew the masses were not likely follow a charlatan.

# 25
## Once I Was Blind

This next miracle came shortly after Jesus had revealed His identity to everyone. As He and His disciples were walking toward Jerusalem, they came upon a man who had been blind from birth. Because it was commonly accepted in those days that sickness and handicaps were usually the consequences of sin, the disciples asked Jesus, "Who sinned, this man or his parents?" (John 9:2).

Jesus answered that neither had sinned. In the case of this man, God had allowed him to be born blind so that Jesus could prove His identity to the world by creating new eyes for him (John 9:3). No one had ever before healed someone who was born blind (John 9:30). A miracle of such enormity would surely prove that Jesus was who He claimed to be.

God didn't cause the man's blindness; nor was He using the poor man as a guinea pig. God used his unfortunate circumstances, though, for His purposes and the man's ultimate joys, both physical and spiritual. Jesus used the circumstances to announce again that He was the light of the world. He was not only the spiritual light for the whole world; He was also going to be the physical light for the blind man.

Without waiting for more questions, Jesus spit on the dusty ground, made a clay paste, and put it on the eyes of the blind man. Then He told him to wash it off in the pool of Siloam. "The man went and washed, and came home seeing" (John 9:7).

The blind man had not seen Jesus. He let Him touch his eyes and then he did what he was told to do. Very simple. Trust and obey. It works every time!

His neighbors and former acquaintances saw the man first. Some thought they recognized him as the former blind beggar. Others thought he merely resembled the beggar. The jubilant man heard their remarks and corrected them, He proudly proclaimed, "I am the man" (John 9:9).

In utter astonishment, the crowd asked him how his eyes were opened. He explained, "The man they call Jesus made some mud and put it on my eyes. He told me to go to Siloam and wash. So, I went and washed, and now I can see" (John 9:11).

The people then asked him where Jesus was. But the man didn't know. He didn't need to see Jesus to believe in Him. Did they? Why couldn't they just join him in his overwhelming joy?

Instead of celebrating with the elated man, the people took him to the Pharisees, because they knew he received his sight on the Sabbath. The Pharisees were peeved once again, but they were also divided in their convictions of Jesus. Some of them said He was not from God, because He did not obey their traditional Sabbath laws. Others shook their heads and asked how a sinner who didn't acknowledge their oral laws could possibly perform such miraculous feats (John 9:16). The wavering Pharisees stooped low enough to ask the man himself what he thought about Jesus.

The man was not concerned about who Jesus was! He was ecstatic over his new ability to see for the first time in his life. He couldn't understand why no one else seemed willing to share his miraculous blessings with him. Jesus? Well, he didn't know much about Jesus, but he was convinced that He must be a prophet (John 9:17).

Some of the Pharisees were determined to label the miracle as a fraud, so they stepped forward and told the crowd they did not believe the man had really been born blind. Therefore, no miracle had occurred; the man must be faking. Then in order to steer away from the truth, the Pharisees sent for the man's parents.

The parents complied with the summons and appeared before the Pharisees. But they didn't commit themselves, because they were afraid of being excommunicated. Being excommunicated meant being shut out of the temple and the synagogue. No one was allowed to speak to or conduct business with people who were excommunicated, so it removed them from everything religious and social. It turned them into outcasts, like lepers. It shut them out of life.

The Pharisees controlled the synagogues, and they had recently made it very clear that anyone who accepted Jesus as the Son of God would be excommunicated. Knowing their plight, the parents told the Pharisees the blind man was indeed their son, who was born blind. But they quickly added, "But how he can see now, or who opened his eyes, we don't know. Ask him. He is of age. He will speak for himself" (John 9:21).

This put the Pharisees in another tight spot. They couldn't deny that a miracle had taken place, so they decided to take any credit away from Jesus by declaring He was a sinner. He wasn't doing things their way. With a new plan in mind, they called the formerly blind man back to their court and told him to give the glory to God for his eyesight ... not to Jesus, because He didn't deserve it (John 9:24).

The man didn't know if Jesus was a sinner, and he probably didn't care that day. He told the Pharisees openly and honestly, "One thing I do know. I was blind, but now I see" (John 9:25). His testimony neither satisfied nor deterred the rulers. They badgered him again to find out just how Jesus had opened his eyes. In exasperation, the man sarcastically replied, "I have already told you, and you did not listen. Why do you want to hear it again? Do you want to become His disciples, too?" (John 9:27).

Of all insults! The Pharisees didn't want to follow Jesus; they wanted to kill Him. They caustically reminded the man that he might be a disciple of Jesus, but *they* were disciples of Moses, who they revered and who they knew had spoken with God. As for Jesus, they sputtered, "We don't even know where He came from" (John 9:29).

The man wasn't going to listen to the rulers a minute longer. He ended his explanations with a sharp retort: "Nobody has ever heard of opening the eyes of a man born blind. If this man were not from God, he could do nothing" (John 9:32, 33).

The Pharisees weren't about to tolerate a commoner's lecture. They thought he was born in sin and was therefore worthless. Even worse, he had sided with Jesus as a man from God, so they excommunicated him.

When Jesus heard the honest man had been thrown out in defense of Him, He intervened. He went to the man and brought him spiritual sight in addition to his physical eyesight. Jesus asked him a crucial question: "Do you believe in the Son of Man?" (John 9:35).

The man replied eagerly, "Who is he, sir … tell me so that I may believe in him" (John 9:36). The man had never seen Jesus, so he didn't recognize Him. But it was obvious he wanted to go further. He wanted to know the Son of Man.

Jesus saw his open, sincere heart and responded warmly, "You have now seen him; in fact, he is the one speaking with you" (John 9:37).

The man knew instantly that he was speaking to Jesus! He knew who He was and what He had done for him. His frustrating experiences with the religious leaders had strengthened his faith and clarified his thoughts. He replied immediately, "Lord, I believe!" (John 9:38). His excommunication wasn't the end of his world after all. It was a beginning! Jesus had led him out of a wayward Judaism into a new Light and a new birth.

This was one of the best examples of pure faith in the entire Word of God. The man learned about Jesus step by step. He opened his heart and mind to Him and received Him as his Lord and Savior. He accepted Him readily and worshipped Him reverently.

The phrase, "Once I was blind, but now I see," is the solid testimony of every sinner who has ever been saved. It is very simple and extremely important. It's the same thing as saying, "Once I didn't know I was a sinner, but now I do … and now I know I need a Savior. Once I was in spiritual darkness … once I didn't know Christ … now I see the Light … now I know Him as my Savior." What a testimony!

Jesus forgives those who accept Him and come to Him to confess their sins. It's the amazing grace. Believers will not get the ultimate punishment they know they deserve. They will not be separated from Him when they die. Their sins will be forgiven, and they will live with Him forever. God doesn't forgive people just so they will be forgiven. He forgives them so they will forgive others.

Jesus explained to the man that He came into this world, "so that the blind will see, and those who see will become blind" (John 9:39). The Pharisees overheard His conversation and knew Jesus was talking about them, so they asked Him if they were blind, too (John 9:40). Jesus basically told them yes, they were spiritually blind. They claimed they could see, but they couldn't, so their guilt would remain (John 9:41).

This story began with a physically blind man, and ended with spiritually blind leaders. The Pharisees said they didn't need a Savior, because they were religious not sinful. They didn't feel spiritually sick, so they weren't interested in a diagnosis or prescription from a physician of the soul. In the presence of Light … in the presence of Christ … in the presence of the revelation of God, the Pharisees didn't see the Truth. They never opened their hearts or minds to Jesus, because they never accepted Him as the Anointed One sent to earth by God.

Jesus could do nothing more for them. He could not save those who continually rejected Him as Lord and Savior. He told them who He was, but they refused to believe Him. Tragically, they were spiritually blind.

# 26
## The Shepherd and His Flock

Jesus not only made it very clear that the religious leaders were blind, He continued to belittle them by presenting His credentials of higher authority. First, He declared Himself to be the Good Shepherd, who had been appointed by God as their Savior and King (John 10:1–21). Then He contrasted Himself with the blind rulers who were self-appointed, self-righteous, and doomed (Ezekiel 34:1–31). They were false shepherds, foolishly leading the flock (the Jewish people) away from the true identity of Jesus and the kingdom of God.

The image of God as a shepherd is used frequently throughout the Bible: "the God who has been my shepherd all my life" (Genesis 48:15); "The Lord is my shepherd, I shall not want" (Psalm 23:1); "He tends His flock like a shepherd" (Isaiah 40:11).

God promised to send other shepherds to lead the Israelites: "Then I will give you shepherds after my own heart, who will lead you with knowledge and understanding" (Jeremiah 3:15). He also warned He would punish the shepherds who did not lead His chosen people according to His standards: "Woe to the shepherds of Israel who only take care of themselves!" (Ezekiel 34:2).

The first-century sheepfold was a public enclosure or pen. The shepherds led their sheep there every evening and turned them over to a watchman for safe-keeping during the night. If they wanted a break from the fields, the shepherds could then spend the night in their own homes and return the next morning. They identified themselves to the watchman and then led their sheep back out to pasture. Unlike Western shepherds today, who often use dogs to drive their sheep from behind or from the sides, the ancient shepherds walked ahead of their sheep and called for them to follow.

When a shepherd went to the sheepfold in the mornings, his sheep were always mixed up with other sheep, but it wasn't necessary to brand or mark them. They didn't have to be identified or checked out, because the watchmen all knew that sheep didn't follow strangers! The sheep knew the voice of their shepherd and wouldn't follow any other shepherd out of the pen. If a shepherd had one hundred sheep in a sheepfold holding one thousand sheep, every one of his hundred would follow him when he called.

Jesus used "sheepfold" as a representation of Israel when He spoke to the religious leaders. He told them He had come into the sheepfold through the gate. He had come in legally, according to Old Testament prophecies. He had been born in Bethlehem, according to prophecy (Micah 5:2). He had been born of a virgin, according to prophecy (Isaiah 7:14). He had also been born into the royal line of King David. He had come through the gate, and He was going to lead His sheep (people) to everlasting life.

Jesus felt sorry for the people. He thought of them as sheep without a shepherd (Matthew 9:36; Mark 6:34) and knew they could not survive on their own.

Sheep are not very intelligent animals. If one goes over a cliff, the entire herd is likely to go over the same cliff. If one strays over a hill and loses sight of the flock, it becomes lost and vulnerable. Sheep have no survival instincts, no means of protecting themselves, and no ability to outrun their enemies. They are helpless without a good shepherd.

Jesus knew the people were following false shepherds who didn't have His credentials and who didn't come into the sheepfold through the gate. The people weren't safe. They were vulnerable. He intended to lead them out of Judaism as they knew it, out of a legal system where they were not being fed the right spiritual food. He would lead them to green pastures beside still waters (Psalm 23).

The religious leaders couldn't understand Jesus' references, because their ears were spiritually blocked. They heard what Jesus said, but they didn't hear it as the Word of God, so they didn't understand His explanations. They didn't hear His voice, because they weren't His sheep!

Unfazed by their dullness, Jesus continued to list His credentials and intentions using His familiar metaphors and allegories. He told the crowd that not only had He come in through the gate, He was the gate! "I am the gate; whoever enters through me will be saved"

(John 10:9). Jesus informed the ones who could hear Him that He is the door of salvation. He is the way out of a troubled life and into a full life. "I have come so that they will have life, and that they might have it more abundantly" (John 10:10).

Jesus was not talking about an abundant life in the next world. He was talking about a good life right here on earth. Salvation is not an escape from this world. It is God's engagement with this world. Jesus was telling anyone who would listen He is the way to the Father ... and He is the *only* way. Those who believe in Him as the Son of God and Savior of the world will be filled with the Holy Spirit, which will make them powerful and joyfully secure. They will gain an abundant life, which others will see and also desire. Jesus gave them a choice: stolen lives and destruction under the oppressive regime of their current blind rulers, or an abundant life under belief in Jesus as the promised Messiah.

Monumental statements ... and He wasn't finished. He galloped on to disclose further intentions: "I am the good shepherd. The good shepherd lays down his life for the sheep" (John 10:11). He was going to die for His followers, but no one was going to take His life from Him. He was going to give it freely. God the Father had given Him the power and authority to lay down His life at His own discretion, and to take it back up again (John 10:18).

Then, to most everyone's astonishment, Jesus announced He was going to die for Gentiles as well as for Jews. His promises would be extended to the entire world. Anyone who heard His voice would be welcome to follow Him—rich and poor, slaves and free, black and white, Jews and Gentiles. One large flock ... and one Shepherd.

With that new revelation, the rulers were divided once again. They believed salvation was for Jews only. Some asked why anyone would listen to a man who was obviously demon possessed and raving mad (John 10:20). Other leaders hedged and said, "These are not the sayings of a man possessed by a demon. Can a demon open the eyes of the blind?" (John 10:21). Some knew He was the Son of God but rejected His leadership, because they wanted to lead. Some acknowledged His awesome power but thought He received it from

Satan, not God. Others argued His messages and miracles were definitely from God. They thought He had been set apart from other leaders because He was holy. He loved God's Word, and He lived God's Word. They were beginning to understand Jesus, because they were beginning to hear His voice. A few religious leaders eventually turned from their ways and followed Him. Why was there such division between the religious leaders? Because some were His sheep, and some were not.

The same division exists today. Jesus is the most controversial man who has ever lived. Either He was a fraud, or He is the Son of God. Either He was a madman who died on a cross, or He is the Savior of the world, who lives to guide His followers. Jesus did not come to this world the first time to bring peace. He came to bring division (Luke 12:51). Some will follow Him. Most will not. "Small is the gate and narrow the road that leads to life, and only a few find it" (Matthew 7:14).

Jesus left Jerusalem and returned in the winter, two months later, for the Feast of Dedication (Hanukkah). The festival commemorates the rededication of the temple after Judas Maccabeus led a successful revolt against the Seleucid (Syrian) ruler Antiochus Epiphanes in about 165 BC. The Judeans regained their independence and kept it for about one hundred years, until Rome (Pompey) took control of Palestine in 63 BC.

When Jesus returned to Jerusalem, the religious leaders gathered around Him once again and asked, "How long will you keep us in suspense? If you are the Christ, tell us plainly" (John 10:24). They were not seeking new clarity regarding who Jesus might be. They merely wanted Him to declare outright in public that He was the Messiah, so they could attack Him with justification. They had been trying to trip Him up for two years, but Jesus had been masterful in avoiding open blasphemy. Instead of representing Himself to be of divine origin, He kept explaining how He didn't bring His own laws into this world, but brought laws in from the One who had sent Him. The leaders worried about that "One" but never considered Him to be the real Father of Jesus.

Jesus was about to change their minds. He responded to their question by reminding them He already had told them exactly who He was. They didn't believe Him, because they weren't His sheep (John 10:26). He told them their rejection of Him was unfortunate, because God the Father was not only the One who had given Him the sheep, but He also stood behind Him to guarantee their protection and eternal security. Since the religious leaders who continually rejected Him were not His sheep, they would not be in line to receive everlasting blessings.

Just as the leaders began to understand His implications, Jesus gave them the words they had been yearning to hear. Very plainly, Jesus stated, "I and the Father are one" (John 10:30).

There it was! A staggering claim actually made in public that Jesus was God. For the third time, the pious Jews picked up stones to hurl at Jesus. But they stopped when He asked why they were accusing Him of blasphemy when He was telling them the truth.

Without waiting for them to answer, Jesus ended the face-off abruptly by commanding, "Even though you do not believe in me, believe the miracles, that you may know and understand that the Father is in me, and I in the Father" (John 10:38). Believe in the water that was changed to wine; believe in a man who can walk on water, still a storm, heal a nobleman's son from a distance, feed five thousand people in one day, and open the eyes of a man born blind!

Too much information! Once again the leaders tried in vain to seize Jesus, and once again, He escaped their grasp (John 10:39).

Jesus was not surprised by their hostile reactions. He expected opposition. He knew they would soon be successful and have Him crucified. But *He* was going to control the circumstances of His death, just as He had controlled every step of His life. He was willing to lay down His life for the sins of the world, but no one was going to take it from Him before He was ready.

# 27
## Lazarus

From Jerusalem, Jesus took His disciples east, across the Jordan River, to a less-populated area known as Perea, which was ruled by Herod's brother, Philip. It was the same area where John the Baptist worked before he was imprisoned and beheaded.

Jesus would no longer reach out to the nation of Israel. He retired to a private ministry and focused on discussing the future with His disciples and friends as He prepared to face His death. In Perea, Jesus continued to heal the sick and teach about the kingdom of God to anyone who came to Him with open hearts (Matthew 19:2; Mark 10:1).

The Pereans were not religious Jews, but they remembered what John the Baptist had taught them about the coming Messiah. Unlike the Judeans, they readily believed in Jesus (John 10:42). They believed that He was exactly who He claimed to be. They believed He was the Son of God, and they trusted in Him for their salvation. They were thankfully delighted to have Him in their midst. Many would follow Him on to Jericho and Jerusalem.

While Jesus was still in this Transjordan area, a messenger arrived to tell Him that His close friend Lazarus was very sick. To everyone's surprise, Jesus did not rush to see him. His disciples were relieved He stayed in Perea, because Lazarus lived in Bethany, which was only two miles from Jerusalem. The frenzied mob there was likely to kill Jesus and His disciples. It was only one day away from where they were, but it wasn't safe.

Two days later, Jesus worried His disciples by announcing, "Lazarus is dead, and for your sake, I am glad that I was not there, so that you may believe. But let us go to him" (John 11:14, 15). Believe what? Believe in Jesus ... more!

Supernaturally, Jesus knew the plight of Lazarus. He knew He was going to raise him from the dead, which would strengthen His disciples' faith in Him as Messiah and Son of God. The Twelve were going to carry His work forward after He was gone, and they would need to stand very tall in front of strong Jewish rejection. His delay ensured that no one could misinterpret His miracle as a fraud or a mere restoration. Everyone knew Lazarus was very dead.

When they arrived in Bethany, at the home of Martha and Mary, disorder prevailed. It was crowded with friends, relatives, and professional weepers, groaners, and wailers. As soon as Martha heard Jesus coming, she ran out to meet Him. She cried, "Lord, if you had been here, my brother would not have died. But I know that even now, God will give you whatever you ask" (John 11:21, 22). Martha knew that Jesus had a special relationship with God and merely hoped He would ask Him for something good to happen.

Jesus told her very kindly that Lazarus would rise again (John 11:23). Martha didn't trust herself enough to fully believe in the resurrection of her brother, or even to hope for it, so she responded with basic faith, and said, "I know he will rise again in the resurrection at the last day" (John 11:24). She knew God's promise from the prophet Daniel: "Go your way till the end. You will rest, and then at the end of the days, you will rise to receive your allotted inheritance" (Daniel 12:13).

With her faithful declaration, Jesus proclaimed, "I am the resurrection and the life … whoever lives and believes in me will never die … Do you believe this?" (John 11:25, 26).

Martha responded immediately: "Yes, Lord. I believe that you are the Christ, the Son of God, who was to come into the world" (John 11:27). Jesus had led her from an abstract belief in the promise of the resurrection that will take place "at the last day" (John 6:40) to a concrete trust in Him as the One who can conquer death and give life at any time. There are no limits of time for the One who has the power of resurrection and life.

Elatedly, Martha hustled back to find her sister, Mary, and to tell her that Jesus was looking for her. Mary left to find Him without hesitating. Some of her friends followed her, thinking she was going to Lazarus's grave, and not wanting her to grieve alone.

When Mary found Jesus, she fell at His feet and said the same thing Martha did: "Lord, if you had been here, my brother would not have died" (John 11:32). Undoubtedly, she and her sister had been lamenting His absence during Lazarus's illness. Mary started to cry. So did the others, and so did Jesus (John 11:35). He didn't weep out loud in hopeless grief like the others, because He knew what He had come to do. But His compassion for their sorrows, coupled with His disappointment in their disbelief in His claims, moved Him to tears, also.

Jesus asked them where they had laid Lazarus to rest and followed them to the tomb. It was a cave with a stone rolled across the entrance to keep out the animals (John 11:38). He told them to move the stone away. They balked, because they knew Lazarus had been there for four days, and the tomb would stink! (Jews didn't embalm bodies like the Egyptians did.) The moaners knew all too well what to expect. Lazarus's body had been wrapped in strips of linen cloth, with plenty of aromatic spices between the layers. But they knew that wouldn't be enough to counteract the repulsive odors from decomposition.

Jesus saw their hesitation and encouraged them to follow His instructions by reminding them that if they believed in Him, they would see the glory of God (John 11:40). That opportunity was too great to reject. If their key to receiving was merely believing, they were ready to comply! They rolled away the stone.

Seeing their actions, Jesus looked up and gave thanks to God the Father: "Father, I thank you that you have heard me. I knew that you always hear me, but I said this for the benefit of the people standing here, that they may believe that you sent me" (John 11:41, 42). Jesus wanted them to know the reason for His next miracle was to authenticate His claims to be the Son of God and the long-awaited Messiah. Who else could raise the dead?

After His prayer, Jesus called out in a loud voice, "Lazarus, come out!" (John 11:43). And Lazarus came out. His hands and feet were still loosely wrapped with strips of linen, and there was a cloth around his face. Jesus told the crowd to take off his grave clothes and let him go (John 11:44).

Raising Lazarus from the dead provided undeniable proof that Jesus had power over death and truly was/is the resurrection and the life. Many of the witnesses present put their full faith in Him. They believed His claims and accepted Him as their Lord and Savior. Others did not. They were the ones who ran off to inform the Pharisees of Jesus' most recent actions.

The Pharisees could not take any judicial action against Jesus by themselves, so they called the Sanhedrin to session. The Sanhedrin was, in effect, the Supreme Court of Israel. It consisted of seventy members who were mostly Sadducees, the religious sect that ran the Jewish temple (the chief priest, the former high priests, and their families). The Sadducees did not believe in resurrection, but the Pharisees did. The Pharisees comprised a minority in the Sanhedrin, but a very influential minority. The Sadducees and the Pharisees were political and religious adversaries, but they were united in their hatred of Jesus.

Caiaphus, the current high priest, took a leading part against Jesus. He said, "It is better for you that one man die for the people, than the whole nation perish" (John 11:50). Why should they sacrifice their whole nation for the sake of Jesus, when they could sacrifice one man for the sake of their nation? His words were very effective. From that day on, the religious authorities began plotting how to take Jesus to the Romans and have Him executed for rebellion against the Empire (John 11:53).

The resurrection of Lazarus marked the end of Jesus' public ministry. It was no longer safe for Him to openly mingle with the Jewish people, so He withdrew to a village near the desert of Judea, which extended to Jericho. It was far enough away from Jerusalem to provide temporary safety until He returned there with His disciples for Passover.

Meanwhile, faithful Jews from other Mediterranean nations flocked to Jerusalem for the preliminary cleansing rituals before the weeklong Passover festival. The chief priests told everyone to watch for Jesus and report His arrival, so they could have Him arrested for rebellion against Rome.

The out-of-towners were surprised by such an edict. They were unaware of the snowballing opposition against Jesus. If they had been leaning toward Him, they kept their allegiances very quiet. They didn't want to be arrested with Him.

The Jerusalem residents in favor of the miracle worker also kept quiet. They didn't want to be excommunicated.

## 28
## Jericho to Jerusalem

When Jesus and His disciples left their desert village for Jerusalem, they passed through Jericho first. The chief tax collector, named Zacchaeus, lived there. He wanted to watch the procession of Jesus and His followers, but he was too short to see. So he climbed a Sycamore tree to catch a glimpse of Him!

When Jesus saw him there, He told him to come down and then invited Himself to a meal at his house. Zacchaeus scrambled down and welcomed Jesus gladly (Luke 19:6). The town residents were upset that Jesus befriended a "sinner" they had rejected from society for exploiting his fellow Jews.

As the chief tax collector in Jericho, a prosperous trading center, Zacchaeus was a very wealthy man. He most likely bid for the right to collect taxes there, and then hired underlings to actually collect the money. But he had not fooled the people. They knew what he did for a living, and they hated him for it. All tax collectors were despised in ancient Israel because they often became rich by pocketing a high percentage of what they demanded. They oppressed the already oppressed.

Jesus understood their feelings, but He knew that social outcasts were also drawn to Him. He also knew the heart of Zacchaeus, which the people had no way of knowing. Jesus told the crowd that He had come to seek and save what was lost (Luke 19:10). Zacchaeus was one of them. He was a son of Abraham, who came to Christ by renewed faith. He wholeheartedly believed that Jesus was exactly who He claimed to be. Zacchaeus was one of the Jews by race, whom Jesus had come to save, and was what He had hoped for when He continually called out, "Repent, for the kingdom of God is near" (Matthew 3:2; 4:17).

To prove that his repentance and conversion was genuine, Zacchaeus gave half his possessions to the poor, even though it was considered generous in those days to give away 20 percent of one's belongings. In addition, Zacchaeus gave back four times the amount of everything he had acquired fraudulently, even though legal restitution for extortion was also only 20 percent (Leviticus 5:16; Numbers 5:7). Zacchaeus had judged his own crimes severely, acknowledged his guilt, and given back far more than required. When he repented, Jesus forgave him. His name was instantly written in the Book of Life.

As Jesus was leaving Jericho, a blind man named Bartimaeus heard the crowd's commotion and asked what was happening. When he learned that Jesus was passing by, he vibrantly called out, "Jesus, son of David, have mercy on me!" (Luke 18:38). The spiritual vision of Bartimaeus was better than the physical vision of most people in the crowd. He cried for mercy, because he fully believed in Jesus' ability to heal him.

Jesus heard him and responded, "Receive your sight; your faith has healed you" (Luke 18:42). Jesus knew genuine faith is the human channel for receiving the gifts of God (Luke 7:50; 8:50; 17:19), so He used the spontaneous reaction of a blind man to highlight the value of belief in Him. Bartimaeus received his sight, praised God, and then followed Jesus. All the witnesses praised God, too (Luke 18:43).

The road from Jericho to Jerusalem was a steep one, which rose about four thousand feet in about twenty miles. It was the last leg of a long journey that began in Caesarea-Philippi. Jesus turned onto it and resolutely set out for the cross. It was also a difficult road, which required more rest stops. Jesus used them to improve the insight of His confused disciples.

Even though Jesus had told them several times what was going to happen to Him in Jerusalem (Matthew 16:21; 17:22, 23), He explained it again: "The Son of Man will be betrayed to the chief priests and the teachers of the law. They will condemn Him to death and will turn Him over to the Gentiles to be mocked, and flogged, and crucified. On the third day, He will be raised to life!" (Matthew 20:18, 19).

Jesus had to make sure His disciples accepted all the grim details and knew there was no Plan B. Nothing was going to change. They knew who He was, but that wasn't enough to save them. They had to understand His full mission. They had to know who He was and what He was going to do for them.

Jesus saw their long faces and knew His disciples were focusing on the unthinkable ... the impending crucifixion of their Messiah. He had never mentioned His death without mentioning His resurrection, but they couldn't seem to step out from under the shadow of the cross. He needed to shift their focus to His resurrection and help them understand that His death without His resurrection would not bring salvation for anyone. It would merely produce another dead person, and His mission would be a failure.

To get His disciples to think about His return rather than His departure, Jesus told them the parable about the ten minas (Luke 19:12–27). "A man of noble birth went to a distant country to have himself appointed king and then to return. So he called ten of his servants and gave them ten minas. 'Put this money to work,' he said, 'until I come back'" (Luke 19:12, 13).

In the first century, kings in Roman provinces (like Galilee and Perea) went to Rome to receive their kingdoms and then returned home. Jesus was preparing His disciples for His departure to receive His kingdom from God the Father. One day, He would return to rule the world. His followers were to love God and each other, and to watch for His return.

On Saturday, six days before Passover, Jesus arrived in Bethany, a suburb of Jerusalem and the hometown of Martha, Mary, and Lazarus, whom Jesus had recently raised from the dead. Community residents hosted a dinner for Jesus, because He had honored their obscure little village with His glorious miracle. Lazarus was the guest of honor. He had become somewhat of a celebrity after the miracle and had drawn small crowds of onlookers who wanted to see the man Jesus had brought back to life.

At the dinner, Mary poured a pint of fragrant oil known as spikenard over Jesus' feet and wiped it up with her hair. It was a display of love for and humble devotion to Him. One of the disciples, Judas Iscariot, objected to her gesture. The oil was an expensive fragrance derived from the roots of a plant grown in India, and Judas thought she had wasted it on Jesus. He thought Mary should have sold it and given the money to the poor (John 12:5).

Jesus came to Mary's defense. He told Judas, "Leave her alone … It was intended that she should save this perfume for the day of my burial. You will always have the poor among you, but you will not always have me" (John 12:7, 8). Jesus knew that Judas had other motives. He didn't really care about the poor. He cared more about money, and he was dishonest. He was the treasurer for Jesus and the disciples, and he used to help himself to their money bag (John 12:6).

When word spread in Jerusalem that Jesus was in Bethany, a large crowd went there to see Him and the man He had raised from the dead. Many of them began to believe Jesus truly was the resurrection and the life. They started backing away from the legalistic religion of the authorities moving toward a genuine faith in Jesus as the Son of God and the Messiah.

Their conversions put Lazarus on the hit list with Jesus. The chief priests were alarmed with the number of crossovers, so they planned to kill them both. They had an additional reason to kill Lazarus. Most of them were Sadducees, who didn't believe in resurrection, and there stood a living refutation of their doctrines! They needed to get rid of Him.

# 29
## So-Called Triumphal Entry
## (Palm Sunday, AD 30)

The next day, Jesus borrowed the colt of a donkey, which had not been ridden yet, and rode it into Jerusalem. It was a royal animal. Religious Jews considered animals that had not been ridden as the only ones suitable for holy purposes (Numbers 19:2; Deuteronomy 21:3; 1 Samuel 6:7). It was also a symbol of peace. Kings rode strong horses to war, but they rode smaller animals when they were at peace. Jesus chose the colt, because He was going to offer Himself to Jerusalem as the king of the Jews and fulfill Zechariah's prophecy in Scripture: "Rejoice greatly, O Daughter of Zion! Shout, Daughter of Jerusalem! See, your king comes to you, righteous and having salvation, gentle and riding on a donkey, on a colt, the foal of a donkey" (Zechariah 9:9).

A large crowd of people went before Jesus and spread their cloaks on the road. It was an act of respect or reverence reserved for high royalty (2 Kings 9:13). Some cut branches from the trees and spread them on the ground. (Palm fronds symbolized joy and salvation.) Others followed Jesus, shouting, "Hosanna to the Son of David! Blessed is He who comes in the name of the Lord! Hosanna in the highest!" (Matthew 21:9). Son of David is a messianic title. *Hosanna* is a Hebrew or an Aramaic prayer that means "save now." Others shouted, "Blessed is the coming kingdom of our father David" (Mark 11:10). They were acknowledging Jesus as the One who was fulfilling prophecy and bringing in the messianic kingdom promised to David's son (2 Samuel 7:12–14; Isaiah 16:15).

These people were not residents of Jerusalem. Most of them were from Galilee and the Judean countryside. Many had followed Jesus from Jericho and Bethany. They knew Him as the One who taught Scripture with authority, healed the sick, cast out demons, and raised the dead. Unlike the twelve disciples of Jesus, these followers had not been convinced that He was actually the Son of Man, the son of David, the Son of God, and their true Messiah. But they knew He was a great prophet empowered by God. That was enough to make Him capable of defeating the detested Romans and establishing Jewish rule worldwide, so they hailed Jesus as King of the Jews and escorted Him into Jerusalem.

Such a huge display of public celebration was rare, and it was the first time Jesus allowed it to happen in His ministry. Before Palm Sunday, Jesus had avoided large crowds in Jerusalem and kept His true identity hushed. Now, though, He was entering Jerusalem in a new role as King! He was forcing Jerusalem to consider His messianic claims and to make a decision. The people in Jerusalem had to accept or reject Him as their Lord and Savior.

What was it going to be? What were the religious leaders going to do with the Son of God? Jesus knew the lamentable answers and gruesome outcome, but He would endure the consequences for their sakes. He still loved them. His imminent death was part of God's great plan for humanity and eternity.

When Jesus finally rode into Jerusalem, the whole city was amazed over the regal procession. The people there asked, "Who is this?" (Matthew 21:10). The others answered, "This is Jesus, the prophet from Nazareth in Galilee" (Matthew 21:11). The residents had certainly heard of Jesus. But few of them accepted His claims of divinity, because the powerful Jewish religious leaders in Jerusalem opposed Him.

Jesus knew Jerusalem sided against Him. He knew the superficiality of the people's hearts. It is why He cried when He approached the city (Luke 19:41). He knew what was going to happen to Jerusalem. The Romans would completely destroy it in forty more years, because its residents and leaders failed to recognize and embrace Him as their Messiah when He offered Himself as their King (Luke 19:44b).

Once Jesus was in the city, the crowds dispersed, and He headed for the temple with His disciples and a few followers. He looked around and saw more unfairness than He wanted to see, but it was getting late. So He returned to Bethany with His band of twelve (Mark 11:11). Bethany was relatively safe, so He stayed there for the next four nights to avoid a premature arrest by the Jewish leaders in Jerusalem.

The Gospels all refer to Jesus' grand procession into Jerusalem as a triumphal entry (Matthew 21; Mark 11; Luke 19; John 12), but there was nothing triumphant about it. Forced into making a decision about Jesus, most of Jerusalem rejected His public presentation of Himself as the Messiah, so His entry ended at the cross, as He knew it would.

Jesus did not come to earth the first time to set up His kingdom. He came to die for it. His entry was not triumphant, but His exit was certainly going to be! It would complete His mission and provide the way for all sins of the world to be forgiven.

Scripture tells us that when Jesus returns to earth the next time, He will appear in glory and touch down on the Mount of Olives (Zechariah 14:4). All nations will bow to Him, and *that* will be His true triumphal entry! It will initiate the millennium and His reign of world peace for one thousand years.

# 30
## Monday

The next morning, Jesus was hungry as He went back to the temple in Jerusalem. He saw a fig tree with leaves on it in the distance and went to see if there might be some figs on it, also. They wouldn't be ripe for another month or so, but He was hoping to find some fruit buds, because they were edible and quite nutritious. When He found leaves only, without figs or buds, He cursed the tree, saying, "May no one ever eat from you again" (Mark 11:14).

Jesus did not condemn the fruit tree out of frustration. He used it as an object lesson for His disciples. The ancient prophets had used the fig tree as a representation of the Hebrew nation (Hosea 9:10; Nehum 3:12; Zechariah 3:10), and Jesus used it to emphasize Israel's spiritual hypocrisy. The nation showed signs of having a God-given religion, but the people weren't exhibiting any spiritual fruit. That was what Jesus condemned!

The fruit of the Spirit is shown by love, joy, inner peace, patience, kindness, goodness, faithfulness, gentleness, and self-control (Galatians 5:22, 23). Neither the people nor their leaders exhibited those attributes. They were becoming the ones God berated through His prophet Isaiah: "These people come near me with their lips, but their hearts are far from me. Their worship of me is made up only by rules of men" (Isaiah 29:13).

Likewise, the people in Jesus' days were going through religious motions and rituals but had little faith in God or power through Him. Their lives had become purposeless. They could no longer demonstrate the vitality or blessings of their lives centered on their one almighty God, because their lives weren't centered on Him.

Since God could no longer use them to set good examples of life with Him, He would use them to set examples of a horrible life without Him. He still loved them, but they had rejected Him and His Son. They were heading toward another catastrophe.

Jesus and His disciples left the fig tree and continued back to the temple, where He had seen corrupt commercialism running rampant in the outer courts. He had overturned the tables of the money changers and driven out all the merchants who were selling sacrificial animals at inflated prices once before, in the early part of His ministry (John 2:13–16), but the merchants had returned to their former practices of extortion.

The temple was supposed to be a center for worship, but it had become a garrison for oppressive bandits, so Jesus drove the "robbers" away again and then turned His attention to the people with real needs (Matthew 21:12–14). He stayed at the temple for the rest of the day. He taught there as usual, and healed all the blind and lame people who came to Him. Afterward, He returned to Bethany for the night.

The growing popularity of Jesus infuriated the religious leaders, who were still searching for a way to get Him killed. They wanted to turn off His "living water" before they drowned in it. They wanted to arrest Him, but they were afraid of His adoring crowds who flocked to Him and hung on all His words.

# 31
## Tuesday

The following morning, Jesus returned to the temple to teach about the kingdom, as He did every day, until He was arrested on Friday. On the way to the temple, Peter exclaimed, "Rabbi, look! The fig tree you cursed has withered!" (Mark 11:20).

Jesus used the dead fig tree as an example of spiritually dead life, stemming from faithless, meaningless prayers. He assured His disciples that they would have better lives with more vitality and power if they learned to pray more efficiently, because the first step toward more productive prayers is more faith in God! The reason they lacked the power to match the mountains of problems in their daily lives was because they lacked the faith that God's will might be done for them one on one. They needed to believe that God could—and would—carry out every one of His promises.

Jesus wanted His disciples to stop trying so hard to please God with senseless rituals and empty prayers. He wanted them to simply believe more in God's infinite abilities to either bless them or judge them, as He had promised! Try less ... believe more ... and connect with God through heartfelt prayers! More faith, more prayers, and more concern for others will always release the vast resources of God's power. Believers will always live better lives than nonbelievers, because their genuine efforts to walk in His ways will always be acknowledged and rewarded.

When Jesus and His disciples reached the temple, the chief priests, teachers of the law (scribes), and elders marched out to Him and challenged His wild actions against the merchants and money changers by asking, "By what authority are you doing these things ... and who gave you authority to do this?" (Mark 11:28).

Their questions were not sincere ones. They didn't want to know the answer. They were merely presenting a dilemma to trap Him in blasphemy or treason. They challenged Jesus because they considered themselves to be the official representatives of religion, and they had not delegated any authority to Him!

Jesus knew their motives and was not about to fall into their trap. Instead, He challenged their assumed authority in public and turned a dilemma back to them by answering their question with one of His own. He said, "I will ask you a question. Answer me, and I will tell you by what authority I am doing these things. John's baptism—was it from heaven, or from men? Tell me!" (Mark 11:29, 30).

It was an excellent question. The religious leaders could not answer it without condemning themselves. If they said, "from men," the crowd would have gone crazy, because the people accepted John the Baptist as a true prophet sent by God, not by men. If the leaders said, "from God," Jesus would have asked them why they didn't believe John. Why hadn't they accepted his messages? Why hadn't they changed their minds and direction?

Caught in a cross fire, the religious leaders wiggled out of their dilemma by feigning ignorance. They simply answered, "We don't know" (Mark 11:33).

Jesus wasn't through with His opposition. He continued fanning the controversial flames by telling them they could reject His messages and kill Him, but they wouldn't be able to destroy the plans of God, because the One they destroyed would become the cornerstone of a new church, which would come back to destroy them.

He explained this to them in the parable of the tenants (Matthew 21:33–44; Mark 12:1–10; Luke 20:9–18). In this parable, a man (God) planted a vineyard (kingdom) and rented it to some vinedressers or tenants (the nation of Israel). Then he went away for a long time. When it was time for the grapes to be harvested, he sent servants (prophets) to collect some of the fruit (profit). The tenants treated all of the servants shamefully. They beat some and killed others. Finally, the man sent his son, thinking the tenants would respect him. They didn't. They knew he was the man's heir, so they killed him, too, hoping to gain his inheritance.

Jesus asked the leaders and the crowd of people what they thought the owner of the vineyard would do to the tenants. Then He answered His own question before anyone responded. "He will come and kill those tenants, and then give the vineyard to others" (Luke 20:16a).

The religious leaders didn't understand the parable. But they were furious, because they knew Jesus had spoken against them. Some of the people in the crowd, though, heard His message and clearly grasped His meaning. They were absolutely stunned and replied, "May this never be!" (Luke 20:16b). They knew that they were God's chosen people and never dreamed He would ever give His kingdom to others. In their minds, salvation was for the Jews, and only for the Jews.

Jesus explained otherwise. New believers in Him would become the caretakers of the vineyard. Jews and Gentiles! "The kingdom of God will be taken away from you and given to a people who will produce its fruit" (Matthew 22:43). The new caretakers would be expected to exemplify good standards of living: reverence for God, consideration for and forgiveness of others, patience, kindness, joy, self-control, faithfulness, and so on.

The kingdom of God would not be permanently removed from Israel. God made promises to Abraham, David, and the prophets that will absolutely not be broken. He promised Jerusalem (Zion) would eventually be restored and rest on the cornerstone of renewed faith in Israel (Isaiah 28:16). Knowing this, Jesus told the crowd He was that cornerstone and applied a messianic verse to Himself, which they all would know: "The stone the builders rejected has become the capstone" (Psalm 118:22). Jesus knew He was going to be crucified in three days and would then become the stone rejected by the builders of the Jewish nation. He would ultimately triumph, though, because the rejected stone of rigid Judaism would become the most significant stone in the new foundation of faith in the kingdom of God (Ephesians 2:20).

Jesus was, and will always be, a stumbling stone for everyone. All people will stumble or fall because of Him (Isaiah 8:14). He told the crowd, "He who falls on this stone will be broken to pieces, but he on whom it falls will be crushed" (Matthew 21:44; Luke 20:18). Believers will stumble over concepts of the new kingdom before submitting their broken pride to Jesus, but they will survive and be rewarded for learning God's will and continually trying to walk in

His ways. Unbelievers will stumble, disregard their bruised egos, and continue to walk in their foolish ways. Eventually, they will be crushed in God's final judgment, when the stone becomes a rock of offense and falls on them (Daniel 2:44, 45).

When Jesus left the temple grounds with His disciples that day, He told them their beloved temple would one day be left "desolate" (Matthew 23:38). Not one stone would be left standing on another (Matthew 24:2). The disciples didn't understand this at all. How could one of the most impressive buildings in the world, with massive stones up to forty feet by twelve feet, by twelve feet again, be destroyed? They went to Jesus privately when He was sitting on the Mount of Olives and asked Him how such a thing could possibly happen. "Tell us ... when this will happen, and what will be the sign of your coming, and of the end of the age?" (Matthew 24:3).

Jesus knew the total destruction of their temple did not fit in with their limited understanding of His return. They still mistakenly thought the kingdom of God was something that was going to happen all at once (Luke 19:11), and that it would somehow be associated with His return to defeat the Romans. They would understand much more about His full mission after His death on Friday and His resurrection on Sunday.

With compassion for their confusion and sorrow for the plight of Jerusalem, Jesus answered most of their questions. He did not tell them when their temple would be destroyed, but He told them how. Even more important, He told them why: "The days will come upon you when your enemies will build an embankment against you and encircle you, and hem you in on every side. They will dash you to the ground, you and the children within your walls. They will not leave one stone on another, because you did not recognize the time of God's coming to you" (Luke 19:43, 44).

This prophecy was precisely fulfilled almost exactly forty years later, in AD 70, when the Roman general Titus built large scaffolds around the walls of the temple buildings, piled them up with wood and other inflammable items, and set them on fire. The heat became so intense that the walls crumbled. The melted gold was collected, and the ruins were tossed into the Kidron Valley below. Later, the site was bulldozed.

The Romans not only demolished the Jewish temple; they destroyed Jerusalem and brutally slaughtered thousands of men, women, and children. Survivors were carried off to be gladiators or other victims of Roman circus games. The utter desolation was God's second judgment against the Jewish people for their failure to recognize and accept their Messiah when He came to visit them. It was similar to God's first judgment against them, when Jerusalem was defeated and leveled by the Babylonians in 586 BC.

Jesus also answered His disciples' questions about His second coming in a lengthy discussion known as the Olivet Discourse (Matthew 24:1–25:46). His answer contains some of the most significant, end-time prophecies in the entire Bible.

Knowing He would not be returning to earth again in the near future, Jesus thoroughly answered their questions about His second coming because He expected His chosen disciples and their successive followers to teach the entire world what to expect before the age of the church comes to an end. He basically told them that wars, diseases, famines, and earthquakes will escalate, Christians will be persecuted, and false prophets will deceive many people. He also revealed there will be an unequaled period of worldwide distress, called the Tribulation, before He returns to judge the unbelievers and make all things right. He concluded His messianic explanations with several parables warning believers to be prepared for His return by using their resources and allowances for His purposes, and to be ever-watchful for His return.

# 32
## Wednesday

The next day, the day before Christ's last supper with His disciples, the chief priests (Sadducees) and the teachers of the law (Pharisees) met to discuss how and when to get rid of Jesus (Luke 22:1). Ideally, they wanted to have Him killed after Passover week, when Jerusalem would not be swarming with thousands of Jewish pilgrims, who had traveled there for one of their three mandatory religious celebrations. The religious leaders all worried about Jesus' adoring fans and agreed that He could not be arrested "during the Feast" because, "there might be a riot among the people" (Matthew 26:5; Mark 14:1, 2).

Judas Iscariot, one of the Twelve, played right into their sinister schemes. (Luke 22:3). He appeared at one of their secret meetings and agreed to betray Jesus. He was willing to reveal where Jesus could be found at night, away from the multitudes. The religious leaders were thrilled to have a traitor fall into their heavy hands, so they paid him thirty pieces of silver for services rendered (Matthew 26:15). Afterward, they dismissed him.

Judas then started to watch for an opportunity to hand Jesus over to the religious authorities.

# 33
## Thursday

Since Jewish days began at 6 p.m. and lasted until 6 p.m. the next day, the Passover meal marked the first day of the eight-day celebration. The entire period was known as either Passover or the Feast of Unleavened Bread. The Passover lambs in Jerusalem were killed on Thursday that week, because the Passover meal there would be eaten that night.

Knowing Judas Iscariot would betray Him as soon as possible after meeting with the religious leaders, Jesus kept the location of His Passover meal a secret until the last moment. When His disciples asked where they would be celebrating that evening, Jesus, in His divine omniscience, told them to follow a certain man in Jerusalem who would be carrying a pitcher of water (Mark 14:13; Luke 22:10). The man would be noticeable, because it was a chore usually carried out by women. When he entered a house, His disciples were to speak to the owner there and say to him, "The Teacher asks: 'Where is the guest room where I may eat the Passover with My disciples?'" (Mark 14:14). Jesus had obviously made prior arrangements with a friend or an acquaintance who had a large, furnished, upper room available for them on short notice.

The disciples found the owner and prepared the meal, not realizing it would be the last one with their Master before His death.

Before eating, Jesus taught His disciples a lesson about humility by washing their feet. Foot-washing before meals was common because of the dusty, dirty conditions of the area, but it was a menial chore and usually performed by slaves. Jesus knew His disciples were still squabbling over which one of them was the most important (Luke 22:24), so He dressed Himself like a slave and showed them there was no pecking order in His kingdom. On the contrary, they were to love one another and serve one another just as He loved and served them. They were embarrassed, but Jesus assured them His service to them was also a spiritual cleansing. Symbolically, He was cleansing them from sin. If they refused His service, they could have no part with Him. None of them protested further.

The Passover meal followed the foot-washing. It was eaten after sunset and had to be completed by midnight (Exodus 12:8–14) It consisted of

(1) Drinking a cup of red wine mixed with water (the cup of thanksgiving)
(2) A ceremonial washing of hands to be spiritually and morally clean
(3) Eating bitter herbs, symbolic of the Israelite's bondage in Egypt
(4) Drinking a second cup of diluted wine, while the head of the household explained the meaning of Passover
(5) Singing two songs of praise to the Lord from the Hallel (Psalms 113–118)
(6) Serving the lamb and distributing the unleavened bread
(7) Drinking the third cup of diluted wine (the cup of blessing)

Before they began the traditions, Jesus predicted His betrayal: "I tell you the truth, one of you is going to betray me" (John 13:21). Flabbergasted, the disciples wondered who would do such a thing. The apostle John asked Him directly, and Jesus answered that it would be the one to whom He offered a piece of bread. With that statement, Jesus dipped a piece of bread in one of the many dishes and handed it to Judas Iscariot. He told Judas, "What you are about to do, do quickly" (John 13:27).

Judas left the room immediately. He knew where Jesus would go after the meal, so he went to inform Caiaphas, the high priest.

Jesus knew that the religious leaders wanted to wait for a more politically opportune time to arrest Him. But they would not be able to postpone their plans, because God's timetable trumped theirs! Passover was God's chosen time for Jesus to sacrifice His life (Matthew 26:2, 18). Just as God had "passed over" and protected the Israelites in Egypt, who had marked their door frames with lambs' blood before the exodus, He is also going to "pass over" all people who accept Jesus Christ as His Son and their personal Lord and Savior. God will protect believers from His wrath against the nonbelievers in the end times.

Jesus was the perfect Lamb of God because He was sinless. He was the only one who could die and take away the sins of the world. But He had to die, because, "without the shedding of blood, there is no forgiveness" (Hebrews 9:22).

In the Old Testament, animal sacrifices were made over and over again to atone for sins (Exodus 30:10; Leviticus 5:9; 6:30; 17:11). The blood of animals did not take away sins, but the sacrifices were necessary to remind people of their sins and to point to the One coming, who would die once and truly take away the sins of the world.

Jesus was in complete control of all His circumstances. He had come to earth the first time as a servant to God and others. Scripture would dictate when He would leave (Matthew 26:54). The Paschal Lamb was going to leave this earth during Passover.

After Judas left, Jesus announced, "I have eagerly desired to eat this Passover with you before I suffer" (Luke 22:15). He knew His disciples were bewildered because He told them He had come from God and was returning to God (John 13:3). He knew they were disheartened because He was going away (John 13:33). He knew they were confused because He told them He was going somewhere they could not follow any time soon, but would definitely follow later (John 13:36b). He wanted to lift their spirits, so throughout their meal together, He prepared them for some of the things that were going to happen during the next twenty-four hours. He comforted them by talking about His return instead of His departure. To top it off, Jesus told them they would soon receive a special gift from God.

First Jesus explained He was going away to prepare a place for them in heaven. He promised to come back and get them, so they could always live with Him (John 14:2, 3). He was not referring to His resurrection, as they thought. He was referring to the Rapture, but He did not expect them to understand that future event quite yet. Saint Paul would reveal the details about it in the years ahead.

Next, Jesus told them more about His coming resurrection and consoled them by saying, "I will not leave you as orphans; I will come to you. Before long, the world will not see me anymore, but you will see me. Because I live, you also will live" (John 14:18, 19).

Finally, to convince His disciples that they would live because He would live, Jesus patiently explained, "I am in my Father, and you are in me, and I am in you" (John 14:20). Nothing was ever going to change. Consequently, since God was going to raise Him back to life, He would also raise His followers who die before His return.

Jesus never mentioned His ascension. His disciples knew nothing about that. Nor would they before it happened, but He prepared them for it anyway. He promised them God would provide them with the Holy Spirit (John 14:15), who would teach them all things and remind them of everything He said and did during their past three years together (John 14:25). Jesus referred to the Holy Spirit as "another Counselor" (John 14:16), a defense attorney for them for life!

Jesus remained calm and collected throughout their last supper. He wasn't looking at the cross. He was looking beyond it to the realm in which He truly belonged. He looked forward to His return to the full glory He had with God the Father before the world began (John 17:5; Genesis 1:26). He wanted His disciples to look beyond the cross, too, but He realized they were still mired in its shadows. All He could do was to explain what was going to happen, so they would understand and believe Him when it did.

In farewell, Jesus left them with a new source of inner strength. He said, "Peace I leave with you; my peace I give to you. I do not give to you as the world gives. Do not let your hearts be troubled and do not be afraid" (John 14:27). This was not the customary good-bye exchange among Jews, who said, "Shalom," which means "peace." Jesus' special grant of peace was personal and supernatural. It was not an absence of conflict. It was the presence of God. It was a divine peace that would allow them not to be afraid. It was a peace that would transcend all their worries and fears. It was a peace unknown to unsaved unbelievers!

Before leaving the upper room, Jesus took a piece of bread, gave thanks, broke it, and gave it to His disciples, saying, "This is my body, given for you; do this in remembrance of me" (Luke 22:19). Then in the same manner, He took a cup of wine and said, "This cup is the new covenant in my blood, which is poured out for you" (Luke 22:20). His death the next day would be poured out for the forgiveness of many sins (Matthew 26:28). He passed the cup around to His eleven disciples, thereby initiating the first communion of saints. Communion simply means to have in common, to participate and have partnership with.

It was definitely a new covenant, because it was going to be ratified with His own blood, unlike the Old Testament covenants, which were ratified with the blood of an animal (Genesis 8:20; 15:9, 10; Exodus 24:8). It was a new promise that Jesus would die on the cross for the remission of all sins. It was the epitome of good news about God's love for humankind. It substantiated the primary gospel truth of Scripture: "For God so loved the world, that He gave His only begotten Son, that whosoever believeth in Him shall not perish, but have everlasting life" (John 3:16 KJV).

With the Lord's Supper, the communion of saints, and the new covenant, Jesus created a new memorial feast in remembrance of Who had delivered believers from sin. He changed the Passover of the Old Testament, which honored God's deliverance of the Israelites from Egyptian slavery, to the Lord's Supper of the New Testament, which honors God's deliverance from sin.

After drinking the wine, they sang another hymn and then walked out to the Mount of Olives (Mark 14:26). There, Jesus told them they were all going to fall away from Him that night because of what was going to happen (Matthew 26:31). Furthermore, there was nothing they could do about their desertion, because it had been prophesied nearly five hundred years ago by God's prophet Zechariah, who said, "I will strike the shepherd, and the sheep will be scattered" (Zechariah 13:7).

Jesus tried to console them so they wouldn't feel ashamed when they abandoned Him. He told them not to worry, because He would not be alone. His Father would be there with Him (John 16:32).

Peter instantly asserted his opinion and boldly declared his loyalty to Jesus. He said, "Even if all fall away on account of you, I never will" (Matthew 26:33).

Jesus countered Peter's ardent denial and said to him, "I tell you the truth … this very night before the rooster crows, you will disown me three times" (Matthew 26:34).

Still truculent, Peter proclaimed, "Even if I have to die with you, I will never disown you" (Matthew 26:35).

Jesus knew Peter's spirit was strong, but his flesh was weak (Matthew 26:41; Mark 14:38). He knew Peter would flee with the others, but He never lost hope in him. He prayed that Peter's faith in Him would not fail and kindly told him that when he turned back, he was to strengthen his brothers (Luke 22:32).

None of the disciples realized that night that their dreams were dying. Their new kingdom was not going to be a mighty restoration of Israel by a powerful Jewish king and his Jewish generals. It was going to be a kingdom of God, led by a carefully chosen but terribly frightened band of disciples.

# 34
## The Arrest of Jesus

Jesus left Jerusalem with His disciples and walked east across the Kidron Valley into an olive garden called Gethsemane, on the Mount of Olives. There He prayed, "My Father, if it is possible, may this cup be taken from me. Yet not as I will, but as you will" (Matthew 26:39).

In the Old Testament, "cup" symbolizes God's wrath against sin (Isaiah 51:17; Jeremiah 25:15). Jesus was not asking for an escape from His impending crucifixion. He accepted the physical suffering as God's will. But He was horrified about facing the separation from His Father when He took the sins of the entire world upon Himself and, thereby, became the object of divine scorn.

After His prayers, Judas Iscariot arrived at Gethsemane with Jewish officials, a detachment of soldiers, and a crowd of armed men. They came to arrest Jesus, and they came prepared to fight. They knew Jesus had supernatural powers and thought He might use them in His defense.

Jesus had no intentions of rebellion. He was ready to surrender, but His disciples didn't know that. When the men stepped forward to seize Him, Peter stepped forward to defend Him. Peter drew his sword and cut off the ear of the high priest's servant. (John 18:10). Jesus rebuked Peter for his vicious retaliation and instantly healed the servant's ear (Luke 22:51). Then Jesus turned to the arresting participants and said, "Am I leading a rebellion, that you have come with swords and clubs? Every day I was with you in the temple courts, and you did not lay a hand on me. But this is your hour—when darkness reigns" (Luke 22:52). With that ominous statement, the twelve disciples deserted Jesus and fled, just as He had predicted (Mark 14:50). They weren't about to hang around in reigning darkness. If armed crowds came for Jesus, they could easily come back for them.

Jesus was bound and taken first to Annas, the political leader of Jerusalem. Annas had been the Jewish high priest from AD 7 to 14 but had been deposed by the Romans. His son-in-law, Caiaphus, was appointed in AD 18 and served the honored position until AD 37. The Jewish religious leaders and soldiers took Jesus to Annas, because they still considered him to be their high priest. According to Jewish law, the high priest is supposed to serve for a lifetime. Annas had been deposed by the Romans but was still honored by the Jews.

Jesus' appearance before Annas was not a true trial. The Sanhedrin was not present. Annas was merely trying to gain more information, such as how many followers had Jesus gained, and what were His doctrines?

Jesus answered that He had not founded any secret organization. He had always taught in synagogues or in the temple and had not said anything in secret sessions. In His own words, "I have always spoken openly to the world" (John 18:20). Jesus then asked Annas, "Why question me? Ask those who heard me. Surely they know what I said" (John 18:12).

An official nearby heard Jesus' reply and slapped Him in the face, because they considered it disrespectful of the high priest. Jesus considered the official's reaction to be inappropriate, so He asked, "If I spoke the truth, why did you strike me?" (John 18:23).

Annas had heard enough! He kept Jesus bound and sent Him to Caiaphus' house, where the Sanhedrin had hastily gathered. This Jewish council *should have* accepted Jesus, exalted Him, and become His publicity agents. Instead, they plotted to kill Him, because He was a threat to their established hierarchy.

The hearing at Caiaphus's house was illegal. Trials involving capital punishment were supposed to be conducted in public at the temple, and criminal trials were not to be held at night. Jesus was being tried after midnight by leaders who all sided against Him, and by false witnesses who lied under oath. Jesus had no defense. "The chief priests and the entire Sanhedrin were looking for evidence against Jesus so that they could put Him to death, but they did not find any. Many testified falsely against Him, but their statements did not agree" (Mark 14:55, 56).

Jewish law required an agreement between two or more witnesses before a person could be condemned (Deuteronomy 17:6; 19:15).

Several people were willing to come forward and perjure themselves, but single witnesses could not be found to provide the legal evidence necessary to indict Jesus.

Caiaphus was becoming more and more annoyed with the pitiful proceedings and couldn't understand why Jesus didn't respond to any of the accusations against Him. He was hoping Jesus would speak up on His own behalf, and possibly incriminate Himself in the process, but Jesus didn't say anything.

Just when sealing the case against Jesus seemed hopeless, two men came forward and said Jesus planned to destroy the temple, because He didn't like the Jewish traditions being taught there. Their testimonies did not agree, but they said that Jesus claimed He would destroy the man-made temple and build another one—not man-made—in three days (Mark 14:58, 59).

Caiaphus couldn't believe such a promising turn of events! Two witnesses were actually talking about the same offense! He prompted Jesus for a response: "Are you not going to answer? What is the testimony that these men are bringing against you?" (Matthew 26:62; Mark 14:60, 61).

Jesus knew He had been misquoted. Earlier in His career, when He had chased the money changers and merchants out of the temple the first time, He told the religious leaders, "Destroy this temple and I will raise it again in three days" (John 2:19). He had been referring to His resurrection, not to a man-made building. What the false witnesses said, however, was so far-fetched and incorrectly applied that Jesus chose to remain silent. It was a silence of innocence, integrity, and faith in His Father. It also fulfilled Isaiah's prophecy: "He was oppressed and afflicted, yet He did not open His mouth. He was led like a lamb to the slaughter, and as a sheep before her shearers is silent, so He did not open His mouth" (Isaiah 53:7).

Exasperated, Caiaphus challenged Jesus, saying, "I charge you under oath by the living God: Tell us if you are the Christ, the Son of God" (Matthew 26:63).

Accepting the oath and the circumstances, Jesus replied, "Yes, it is as you say … But I say to all of you; in the future you will see the

Son of Man sitting at the right hand of the Mighty One and coming on the clouds of heaven" (Matthew 26:64).

*That* was the statement that convicted Jesus! He was claiming to be the judge of the Jewish people with God's authority, and He referred to Jewish Scripture that described His regal enthronement: "The Lord is at your right hand ... he will judge the nations ... and crush the rulers of the whole earth" (Psalm 110:5, 6).

All Caiaphus heard was Jesus' affirmation of deity and His claim of a relationship to God in which He exercises authority like God's. Caiaphus tore his robes in a phony display of grief; high priests were forbidden to tear their robes unless they witnessed a blasphemy. Then Caiaphus asked the Sanhedrin, "Why do you need any more witnesses? You have heard the blasphemy. What do you think?" (Matthew 26:65, 66).

The Sanhedrin, being little more than a puppet government determined to keep peace at any cost for their Roman masters, quickly answered, "He is worthy of death" (Matthew 26:66). Jesus certainly wasn't the Messiah they wanted, and He was likely to get them all killed if the commoners flocked to Him and the Romans felt threatened.

Caiaphus charged Jesus with blasphemy, because He claimed to have equal power with God. Such a claim in his eyes, was not only preposterous, it was irreverent of God. It was the boast of either a liar or a crazy person.

In God's eyes, however, Jesus had spoken the truth. He was fully human, fully God—and had been since the day He was born in Bethlehem. The Sanhedrin had condemned an innocent man.

Once Jesus had been condemned, the Jewish leaders spat in His face, a gesture considered to be the epitome of all disgraceful insults (Numbers 12:14). In addition, the soldiers mocked Him by playing a horrible game of "Hot Hands" with Him, in which they blindfolded Him, beat Him mercilessly, and then jauntily asked Him to use His prophetic powers to reveal which of them had actually done the hitting (Luke 22:63,64).

# 35
## Peter's Denial

When Jesus was arrested at Gethsemane, a small crowd followed Him first to Annas's house and then to the house of Caiaphus. Peter followed, too, but from a distance. He didn't want to be recognized and possibly arrested.

It was chilly that night, and Peter joined some of the others to warm himself by a fire made in Caiaphus's courtyard. While he was seated there, a servant girl recognized him and said, "You also were with Jesus of Galilee" (Matthew 26:69).

Peter denied it, and replied, "I don't know what you're talking about" (Matthew 26:70). Then he walked away to the gateway.

Another of Caiaphus's servants saw him there and said to the people around her, "This fellow was with Jesus of Nazareth" (Matthew 26:71).

Peter denied his association with Jesus again, and told her, "I don't know the man!" (Matthew 26:72). His accent, though, must have given him away, because a little while later, another man said, "Certainly this fellow was with him, for he is a Galilean" (Luke 22:59).

Peter replied a third time: "Man, I don't know what you're talking about!" (Luke 22:60). Just as he was speaking, two things happened. A rooster crowed, and Jesus looked straight at Peter from an open window in the courtyard (Luke 22:60, 61). Jesus had heard his denials. Realizing he had caved in to his worst fears, Peter broke down and cried (Mark 14:72).

# 36
## Judas Hangs Himself

Early that morning, after the Sanhedrin, the elders, and the teachers of the law had reached a decision to put Jesus to death, they bound Him and took Him to Pilate, the Roman governor of Judea, Samaria, and Idumea (Matthew 27:1,2; Mark 15:1,2).

When Judas Iscariot realized that Jesus had been condemned, "he was seized with remorse" (Matthew 27:3). Knowing he had betrayed an innocent man, Judas threw his thirty pieces of silver back at the chief priests and elders in the temple. Then he went out and hanged himself (Matthew 27:5). Genuine remorse or godly sorrow would have led Judas to repentance and ultimate forgiveness, but his remorse wasn't genuine. His stinging pangs of guilt were genuine, though, and they drove him to a ghastly suicide.

# 37
## Jesus before Pilate

Jesus was condemned by the Jewish court system, but Roman law did not allow Jewish citizens to order the death penalty. Seeking that sentence, the religious leaders took Jesus to Pontius Pilate. Pilate lived in Caesaria, on the Mediterranean coast, but he always went to Jerusalem for the major Jewish festivals.

The seventy members of the Jewish council agreed that Jesus deserved to die for blasphemy, which was a violation of their Mosaic law, but they knew it wouldn't carry any weight in a Roman court. So they changed their charges against Jesus to treason when they took Him to Pilate. They told Pilate Jesus was guilty of perverting the nation, opposing payment of taxes to Tiberius Caesar, and claiming to be a king (Luke 23:2).

Pilate was not concerned about the first charge, because disturbing the peace was not a capital offense. The second charge was an outright lie! Jesus specifically told the people they must render to Caesar what is Caesar's and render to God what is God's (Luke 20:25). The third charge, though, was a direct challenge against Roman authority, so Pilate summoned Jesus inside his palace to find out if He was a possible opposing force. Pilate asked Jesus directly, "Are you the king of the Jews? What is it you have done?" (John 18:33, 35).

Jesus answered, "Yes, it is as you say" (Luke 23:3). He told Pilate that He was the King of the Jews but no threat to Rome, because His kingdom was "not of this world" (John 18:36a). His kingdom would come, but not from a revolution, because the people in Israel were not going to oppose His arrest (John 18:36b).

Jesus never had any intentions of leading a revolt against the Romans, because they were not the problem. The Jewish religious leaders were the major oppressors of God's people (Luke 11:46). They didn't practice what they preached (Matthew 23:3). They only had eyes for themselves and their own interests (Matthew 23:5, 25). On the outside, they appeared to be righteous, but on the inside, they were full of hypocrisy and lawlessness (Matthew 23:28). They were not helping the people; they were misleading, mistreating, and exploiting them. They were making their lives miserable.

Jesus had tried to appeal to the eyes and hearts of the leaders, but they only saw Him as a threat to their authority and leadership. He knew His efforts would not be enough to save the souls of the self-indulgent ones, but He would die trying.

Pilate was greatly consoled that Jesus was not a volatile insurrectionist. He no longer considered Him a serious threat against Roman political power. He went outside to the crowd and announced, "I find no basis for a charge against this man" (Luke 23:4).

The priests were disappointed and determined to convince Pilate otherwise. They knew Pilate had come to Jerusalem to keep an eye on the enormous crowds that flocked there for Passover, and they cleverly maneuvered him to do their dirty work. They told Pilate Jesus was a rabble-rouser: "He stirs up the people all over Judea by his teaching. He started in Galilee, and has come all the way down here" (Luke 23:5). They also warned Pilate he might lose his job in Palestine if the Roman authorities thought he was being derelict in his peace-keeping responsibilities.

Pilate was most relieved to hear that Jesus was a Galilean. That put Him under the jurisdiction of Herod Antipas, who had also come to Jerusalem for Passover. Hoping to get off the hook, Pilate sent Jesus to Herod. Let Herod sentence the innocent man to death!

Herod was excited to finally meet Jesus in person. He was hoping Jesus would perform one of His grand miracles for him. He asked Jesus many questions, but Jesus never responded (Luke 23:9). It would have been pointless for Jesus to answer, because Herod didn't believe in any power greater than the Herod family dynasty, which once ruled all of Palestine on behalf of the Romans. Herod had tried to kill Jesus during the first part of His three-year ministry (Luke 13:31), just as his father, Herod the Great, had tried to kill Him shortly after His birth in the manger (Matthew 7:13).

Jesus considered Herod Antipas to be an old "fox" (Luke 13:32), who had gone past the point of no return. Herod was doomed, because he had always opposed Him and never acknowledged, much less praised, the one God Almighty. Since Herod was a ruthless leader on the way to an eternity for the lost, Jesus made no further effort to reach him.

When Jesus failed to cooperate, Herod mocked Him by dressing Him in an elegant purple robe. It was a sarcastic gesture to His claims of being a king. Then Herod sent Him back to Pontius Pilate.

Pilate was back on the hook. Jesus was now saying nothing, and the Jewish religious leaders were demanding the death penalty for a mere troublemaker. Pilate thought he knew a way out of his political dilemma. He was well aware that the Jewish leaders had not brought Jesus to him out of their allegiance to Rome. They were simply jealous of His increasing popularity with the commoners. They wanted to get rid of Jesus, because He was a direct threat to their hierarchy and positions. Remembering how the people had hailed Jesus as King when He entered Jerusalem on a colt just a few days ago, Pilate knew a legal way to release Jesus to His adoring supporters. He would grant Jesus amnesty.

Ancient custom allowed Roman governors to occasionally grant amnesty to a prisoner at the request of the people. Pilate assumed the people would ask for their acknowledged King to be released, and when they did, their wish would be his command. Little did he know that the chief priests and elders had already persuaded the crowd to ask for another prisoner, Barabbas, to be released and for Jesus to be executed (Matthew 27:20).

When Jesus was returned from Herod's palace, Pilate called the people together with their chief priests and elders. He announced to them, "You brought me this man as one who was inciting the people to rebellion. I have examined him in your presence, and have found no basis for your charges against him. Neither has Herod, for he sent Him back to us. As you can see, he has done nothing to deserve death. Therefore, I will punish him and release him (Luke 23:13–16).

Much to Pilate's surprise, they all cried out, "Away with this man. Release Barrabas to us!" (Luke 23:18).

Pilate didn't listen to them. Pilate sent Jesus to be flogged to create sympathy for him. He was hoping the crowd would feel sick about an innocent man having to suffer through such an awful beating and demand His immediate release.

Flogging, or scourging, was a severe punishment that often killed the victim. An expert flogger used a whip made of multiple leather strands attached to a wooden handle. A sharp piece of bone or metal was attached to the end of each strand. The victim was tied to a post, with his hands high over his head to stretch the skin on his back. Flogging not only tore flesh; it lacerated muscles and often injured internal organs.

Jesus survived the inhumane torture, and Pilate presented Him to the crowd as a victim of injustice, not as the dangerous man the rulers made Him out to be. The guards had beaten and flogged Him. He was bruised, bloody, and miserable. Pilate expected the people to wince. Instead, they yelled for Him to be crucified (John 19:6). The leaders shouted, "If you let this man go, you are no friend of Caesar" (John 19:12).

With one last attempt to free Jesus, Pilate asked the crowd, "Shall I crucify your king?" (John 19:15b).

The chief priests promptly replied, "We have no king but Caesar" (John 19:15c). The crowd kept repeating their demands, louder and louder. They were launching into an uproar, and Pilate couldn't believe what he was hearing. The same people who spread their cloaks and cried hosannas for the Son of David were now crying out for His crucifixion. They had expected Jesus to "save now"! They had expected Him to use His awesome powers to toss out the Romans and set up His new kingdom of worldwide Jewish rule. When it didn't happen, they rejected Him and cried out for His death. They didn't want a spiritual kingdom of peace. They wanted a physical kingdom of might. They wanted Pilate to release an anti-Roman insurrectionist. They wanted Barabbas!

The chief priests had very effectively switched their focus from a religious charge of blasphemy to a political charge of treason. They had forced Pilate to think about his fate if he sided against Caesar and to back away from his innate sense of right.

Pilate didn't have to think very long. He wanted to keep his job! But knowing he was going to be responsible for sending an innocent man to his death, He tried to wash his guilt away publicly. He took a bowl of water and washed his hands in front of all the people. Then he said, "I am innocent of this man's blood … It is your responsibility" (Matthew 27:24).

The people answered, "Let his blood be on us and on our children" (Matthew 27:25). The Jewish officials had instigated Jesus' death, and the people approved it. None of them held the Romans responsible or accountable for the crucifixion.

Unjustifiably absolved, Pilate folded under pressure and handed Jesus over to be crucified.

# 38
## Crucifixion

After Pilate sentenced Jesus to die by crucifixion, the Roman soldiers led Him away to a palace, where they were allowed to do anything they wanted to Him. They were brutal. They repeatedly struck His head with a thick reed, much like a broom handle. They spat on Him. They dressed Him in another purple robe, jammed a crown of long thorns on His head, and then bowed before Him in mock worship. They forced Him to carry His cross in humiliation. Then they led Him away to Golgotha, which means "The Place of the Skull" (Mark 15:22).

Because Jesus had been so severely beaten and flogged, He was only able to carry His cross to the city gates. (Some crosses weighed up to two hundred pounds.) Thinking Jesus might die before the crucifixion, the soldiers randomly chose a man, Simon, out of the crowd and ordered him to help Jesus carry His cross the rest of the way.

When they arrived at Golgotha (Calvary), they offered Jesus a drink of wine mixed with myrrh to help deaden the pain of being nailed to the cross. Jesus refused it (Mark 15:23). He wanted to be in full control of all His faculties until the moment He died. He still had things to say.

Crucifixion was the cruelest form of execution. It was passed down to the Romans from the Persians, Phoenicians, and Carthagenians and was reserved for the worst criminals and all insurrectionists. Though the Romans did not develop it, they perfected the art of its slow torture. The wounds through the victim's hands and feet were not fatal, but they became increasingly unbearable as the hours dragged on. Most victims hung in agony for two or three days and suffered from exhaustion, dehydration, traumatic fever, and attacks from birds of prey before dying. When their legs could no longer support their bodies, they died of suffocation. Breathing was impossible with compressed diaphragms. That's why soldiers broke the legs of victims if they were ordered to hasten their deaths (John 19:31–33).

No gory details of Christ's misery on the cross can be found in the Bible. God did not inspire Matthew, Mark, Luke, or John to describe any of the gruesome facts. They were too horrible. All we learn from Scripture are a few incidents that happened around the cross.

Jesus was nailed to the cross and lifted up at 9 a.m. "It was the third hour when they crucified Him" (Mark 15:25). The Jewish hours began at 6 a.m. His followers, and all of His chosen apostles except John, had fled. Only the women remained faithful until the very end.

Mary, the mother of Jesus, was there at the foot of the cross. Most of the other women who had followed Him all the way from Galilee (Matthew 27:55) watched from a distance. They couldn't bear to watch Him suffer, but they couldn't leave Him, either. The leaders of this loyal group were Mary Magdalene, who became a devoted follower after Jesus delivered her from seven demons; another Mary, the mother of the apostle called James the Younger; and Salome, the mother of apostles James and John, the sons of Zebedee (Mark 15:40).

When Jesus looked down and saw His mother and His disciple John, He said, "Dear woman, here is your son." To John He said, "Here is your mother" (John 19:26, 27). From that day on, John kept the mother of Jesus in his home and cared for her as long as she lived.

Jesus' crime was inscribed on a board and fastened to the cross above His head. Pilate had ordered it to read: "Jesus of Nazareth, King of the Jews." It was written in three languages: Hebrew, the language of Jewish religion; Greek, the language of culture and education; and Latin, the language of law and order (government and military).

The sign enraged the Jewish authorities, who had never accepted Jesus as their king! They wanted Pilate to change it to read, "Claimed to be king of the Jews," but Pilate refused (John 19:22). The religious leaders had given him nothing but trouble, and he didn't care if they were affronted!

People hurled insults at Jesus while He was on the cross. They said things like, "So! You who are going to destroy the temple and build it in three days, come down from the cross and save yourself!" (Mark 15:29). Political leaders and religious rulers also mocked Him, declaring, "He saved others, but he cannot save himself! (Mark 15:31). This was empty mockery. He could have come down from the cross, and it still wouldn't have made any difference to them. He was not the mighty Messiah they wanted. Even after hearing about His extraordinary miracles, the chief priests and teachers of the law chose not to believe Jesus was the Son of God. Empowered by God, perhaps, but not the Son of God and certainly not God-incarnate. They were experts in Scripture, and the prophetic signs all pointed to Jesus, but His kingdom just wasn't complementing their hierarchy. He was way too controversial for all of them. He didn't accept their code of conduct or their management of the people. His death would be a good riddance!

Jesus was ridiculed by almost everyone—Pilate, Herod, the people, the soldiers, the leaders, and even the two thieves who were crucified beside Him. Both thieves heckled Him at first. But one of them acknowledged His innocence much later that day.

These two men were not common thieves. Robbery was not a capital offense under Roman law, so they probably had been involved in an anti-Roman insurrection with Barabbas, who was described as both a robber (John 18:40) and a murderer (Luke 23:18, 19).

Jesus hung on the cross for six hours. He suffered at the hands of humankind for the first three hours and for the sins of humankind during the last three hours.

At noon, the sun stopped shining (Luke 23:45): "From the 6th hour to the 9th hour darkness came over all the land" (Matthew 27:45). This was a supernatural darkness. It was not an eclipse. Eclipses don't last for three hours. Furthermore, ancient Jews used a lunar calendar and always planned Passover on a full moon. A solar eclipse would have been impossible. God made it dark. Humans are very limited in their perception of the spiritual world, so God shut humankind out of a spiritual misery it could not possibly understand.

Sometime during this darkness, one of the two thieves realized that something very unusual was happening. There seemed to be some kind of transaction going on between God and the Man on the cross beside him. When the other thief continued to taunt Jesus, the enlightened one rebuked him, and then asked Jesus to remember him when He came into His kingdom. Jesus replied, "I tell you the truth, today you will be with me in paradise" (Luke 23:43).

About 3 p.m., Jesus cried out, "My God, my God, why have you forsaken me?" (Matthew 27:46). It was an intense cry of spiritual agony. He was quoting Scripture (Psalm 22:1), and He knew the answer. He had been perfect before the cross, and He had enjoyed His relationship with His Father. But as He became sin for the entire world, He felt the wrath of God being poured out on Him and keenly felt abandoned when God the Father looked away. This was the cup He had dreaded, the part of His mission He knew would hurt the most. Please, "take this cup from me" (Luke 22:42). Please don't look away.

Jesus had two more statements to make before dying, but dehydration was making speech very difficult. So He called out, "I am thirsty" (John 19:28). The soldiers soaked a sponge in a jar of wine vinegar and lifted it to his lips on a long stalk of a hyssop plant. It tasted awful, but it provided enough moisture for Jesus to call out in a loud voice, "Father, into your hands I commit my spirit" (Luke 23:46). And then, "It is finished" (John 19:30a). With that final statement, He bowed His head and gave up His spirit (John 19:30b).

*What* was finished? His full mission, His redemption of the world He had provided a way for all believers to join Him in paradise.

The moment Jesus died, there was an earthquake, and the massive curtain in the temple in Jerusalem was torn in two from top to bottom. This curtain sealed the entrance to the Most Holy Place, where God dwelled (Hebrews 8:3; Exodus 26:33). It separated humans from God. Only the high priest could venture beyond this curtain, and only once a year, on the Day of Atonement (Yom Kippur). Anyone else who entered the Most Holy Place would die (Leviticus 16:2).

God did not dwell there in person. God the Father was, is, and always will be a spirit. King Solomon, who built the temple, emphasized that the Lord of the universe could never fully dwell in a building, but His spiritual presence or "name" would always live there in Jerusalem (1 Kings 8:27–30).

No person could have torn this veil. It was too large, too thick, and too heavy. God tore it to end the separation between Him and humanity. The torn curtain signified immediate access to Him, made possible by the death of His Son (Hebrews 10:19,20). Neither priestly sacrifices nor animal sacrifices would ever be necessary again.

Jesus had known He would become the sole mediator for His Father. That's why He taught His disciples that He is "the way, the truth, and the life. No one comes to the Father except through me" (John 14:6).

Non-Christians today hate that verse, because it excludes them. But it is so very true. There is one God and one Mediator now between God the Father and humankind, and His name is Jesus Christ (1 Timothy 2:5). Those who do not believe that Jesus Christ is the Son of God, who died for us on the cross, will have no access to God the Father (1 John 2:23). Nonbelievers will be excluded from an eternal life with God if they continue to reject Jesus as His Son.

The centurion in charge of the crucifixion was a Roman soldier. He didn't worship God the Father or God the Son, but like the thief next to Jesus, the guard knew there was something extraordinarily remarkable about this execution. He heard all the ridicule about Jesus being the Son of God. He saw the darkness fall for three hours. He heard Jesus tell the robber next to Him that he would be in paradise with Him that very day. He had seen many crucified victims die, but none like Jesus, who was so much stronger than all the others. Most victims struggled horribly at the very end of their lives. They made a huge effort to take their last breath. It was an awful, congested gasp known as a death rattle. Not Jesus, though. He cried out in a loud, clear voice and then simply dismissed His spirit. He was in complete control of His circumstances and gave up His life willingly.

The centurion, as well as all the guards, were terrified by all the events, especially the earthquake and reports of the torn veil. They were Roman pagans, who always believed in multiple gods and goddesses, but the one God Almighty had opened their eyes. With new hearts and new faith, they exclaimed, "Surely this man was the Son of God!" (Matthew 27:54; Mark 15:38).

# 39
## The Burial

After Jesus was pronounced dead, a rich man named Joseph asked Pilate if he could bury Jesus in his own tomb, which he had cut out of rock for himself and his family (Matthew 27:60). Pilate agreed and gave the body to him.

Joseph was from Arimathea, a town about twenty miles north of Jerusalem. He was a member of the Sanhedrin but didn't agree with their convictions against Jesus or their desire to kill Him. His request was extremely risky, because it identified him as a follower of Jesus, in direct opposition to the prominent ruling council.

Joseph was assisted by Nicodemus, another member of the Sanhedrin. Nicodemus was a highly respected Pharisee and a teacher of the law, who also came forward to help prepare Jesus' body for burial.

Jews did not embalm bodies like Egyptians did, but they did use spices to counteract the stench from decomposition. Joseph and Nicodemus wrapped Jesus' body in expensive linen cloth and added pounds of myrrh and aloes in the layers and folds, which held them together like glue (John 19:39, 40). When the mixture set up, it would seal out the air. They wrapped His head separately. They had to hurry because of the approaching Passover, which would begin at 6 p.m. that night (Friday) and end at 6 p.m. on Saturday. They would only have a couple more hours to work.

The next day (Saturday), the chief priests and the Pharisees went to Pilate and told him Jesus had informed His followers that He would rise from the dead three days after He was killed. The religious leaders worried Jesus' disciples would steal His body and claim He had been resurrected. To prevent any such thing from happening, Pilate ordered the tomb to be sealed and guarded by soldiers (Matthew 27:66).

# 40
## Resurrection and Ascension

The next day (Sunday), Mary Magdalene, another Mary (mother of James and Joseph), and Salome (mother of disciples James and John) left their homes at dawn to visit the tomb. They were followed by other women bringing more burial spices. Apparently Joseph and Nicodemus had not had enough time to finish their preparations.

When the women arrived at the tomb, there was an earthquake. An angel of the Lord appeared, who rolled back the stone for them to see inside. The dazzling bright appearance of the angel and his awesome power to remove the stone terrified the Roman guards, and they fainted! They "shook and became like dead men" (Matthew 28:4).

The women were also frightened, but the angel comforted them, saying, "Do not be afraid, for I know you are looking for Jesus, who was crucified. He is not here; He has risen, just as He said. Come and see the place where He lay. Then go quickly and tell His disciples" (Matthew 28:5).

Mary Magdalene left and found the disciples, but they did not believe what she told them. Peter and John hurried off to the tomb to see for themselves. They did not believe Jesus had been resurrected until they looked in and saw that the linen wrappings were perfectly intact, but the body was not inside. Even the burial cloth that had been wrapped around His head was folded up by itself and lay separate from the linen (John 20:17). They knew instantly that Jesus had been resurrected after all! His body had risen from a carefully wrapped and sealed encasement without the linen being unwound. Jesus had come forth in a glorified body that was not subject to the laws of universal physics.

Meanwhile, the chief priests, who didn't believe in resurrection, met with the Jewish elders. Together they fabricated a story and came up with a devious plan. They paid the soldiers to lie. They offered them a large amount of money to tell everyone that Jesus' disciples came during the night and stole his body while they were sleeping

(Matthew 28:13). Furthermore, knowing the guards could face a firing squad for losing the body of Jesus because they had fallen asleep on duty, the authorities promised to protect them from a death sentence (Matthew 28:14).

The soldiers accepted the bribe and followed directions. Sadly, their lies have been widely circulated and accepted by Jews to this very day (Matthew 28:15). Misguided but satisfied with their convictions, the majority of faithful Jews have never bothered to ask God to reveal the truth about the disappearance of Jesus' body, or the reports of His appearances after His resurrection.

As infallible proof of His resurrection, Jesus remained on earth for forty days. He showed Himself to many people and continued to teach about the kingdom of God (Acts 1:3 KJV). None of His appearances were made to nonbelievers. They would not have believed He was their Messiah if He had crawled down off the cross and stood before them. To them, He was just a carpenter from Nazareth and a troublemaker for their religious leaders. Jesus knew His disciples would be able to save some of their souls later, with the help of the Holy Spirit, but there was nothing more He could do for those who still rejected Him at that time. Instead, He focused on His followers and those who had seen His death, resurrection, and imminent ascension. All of His postcrucifixion appearances were made to people chosen by God (Acts 10:41). They were the ones who would spread the truth about who He was and what He really came to do.

In His teachings, Jesus linked His death and resurrection to His invisible kingdom. But neither His disciples nor the multitudes could grasp the connection. Every time they heard Him speak about the kingdom of God, it ignited their dreams of a newly restored Israel, with strong armies, shining armor, the unity of King David, the wisdom and wealth of King Solomon, and a chicken in every pot.

Jesus did not rebuke them, because He knew they had been raised and schooled by the laws of Moses and the true prophets. They connected the coming of the kingdom with the coming of the Messiah and the Spirit because of lessons they learned from their religious scrolls (i.e., Ezekiel 39:27–29; Joel 2:28–32; Zechariah 12:8–10). They understood that their Messiah would be the one to establish their kingdom on earth. They were right, but they didn't know He would come twice, because neither Moses nor the ancient prophets had known it either. Throughout the Bible, God progressively reveals more mysteries. We will all learn more as we draw closer to the Second Coming.

Jesus knew His chosen disciples would be able to assemble more pieces of prophecy with what He had said and done during His ministry on earth after His ascension. Then they would teach their revelations of His new covenant (Luke 22:20) to others, and His messages would be carried on in much greater strides.

There are at least ten distinct appearances described in the Bible between the resurrection and ascension of Jesus Christ. He seemed to appear at will in casual settings. No pomp or circumstance.

Mary Magdalene was the first person to see Jesus after His resurrection (Mark 16:9). After finding the disciples to relay the angel's message, she returned to the tomb, not understanding what had happened to His body. When someone asked her why she was crying, she thought the question had come from the gardener, so she asked him if he had taken the body somewhere. She didn't realize she was talking to Jesus until He called her by name: "Mary" (John 20:16).

When she recognized Him, she called out, "Rabboni," which means "teacher" in the Aramaic language He spoke. She raced back to His disciples to tell them she had actually seen Jesus and had spoken to Him. They still didn't believe her, but their convictions no longer mattered. She was overjoyed, knowing He was truly alive and back with them.

That same day, Jesus appeared to the other women who were returning from the empty tomb (Matthew 28:9, 10), to Simon Peter (Luke 24:34), and to two of His other followers, who were on the road to Emmaus, about seven miles from Jerusalem (Luke 24:13–32).

As these two believers were discussing the events of the week and the rumors of that Easter Sunday, Jesus appeared and walked along beside them, and joined in on their conversation. They noticed Him, but like Mary, they did not recognize Him. "Their eyes were held, that they should not know him" (Luke 24:16 KJV). God kept them from recognizing Him, but they casually accepted the friendly stranger in their midst. They told Him how crushed they were over the crucifixion of Jesus. They had hoped He actually was their true Messiah and been waiting for Him to establish His earthly kingdom. And now they thought He was dead. They had heard rumors that day about His resurrection, but they didn't really believe He had come back from the dead. They weren't sure about anything that was happening.

Jesus reprimanded them for not believing their prophets and Scriptures: "Did not the Christ have to suffer those things and then enter His glory?" (Luke 24:26). He proceeded to give them a history lesson by going back to Old Testament Scriptures and explained what Moses and all the prophets had said about the suffering, death, and resurrection of the Messiah.

Fascinated by the stranger's wisdom, the two followers begged Him to stay longer. He graciously complied. At mealtime, Jesus made a familiar gesture when He took the bread, gave thanks, broke it, and began to give it to them. They saw the light. It was Jesus! "Their eyes were opened and they recognized him, and he disappeared from their sight" (Luke 24:31). God had intervened to keep them from recognizing Jesus until it was time for Him to vanish. Surely that is why Mary had not recognized Him at first, either.

The two men immediately returned to Jerusalem to tell the chosen disciples that the rumors of Christ's resurrection were definitely true. Jesus had risen and spent a good part of the day with them. They had no doubt that Mary and Simon Peter had both seen Him, too. Try as they might, the followers from the road to Emmaus were unable to convince the others that Jesus was back and walking with them again (Mark 16:13). They were still confused and divided.

When the two men left, the rest of the chosen disciples remained in the house behind locked doors, still afraid of what the Jewish leaders might do to them (John 20:19). Thomas was not present (John

20:24). While they were rehashing the incredible events and reports, Jesus suddenly appeared and stood among them (John 20:19; Luke 24:36). "He rebuked them for their lack of faith and their stubborn refusal to believe those who had seen him after he had risen" (Mark 16:14).

Jesus had terrified His disciples by appearing out of thin air in the room with them. They thought He was a ghost, not their Master of the past three years in person. Jesus asked why they doubted Him, showing them the nail marks on His hands and feet. Then He declared, "It is I myself! Touch me and see; a ghost does not have flesh and bones as you see I have" (Luke 24:39).

The disciples were not completely convinced. They were enormously delighted to have Jesus back with them, but they still thought He was a ghost. A friendly ghost perhaps, but one who could glide through walls. They didn't think much of being led by an apparition.

To prove He was not a ghost, Jesus asked them for something to eat, since ghosts don't eat food. His disciples gave Him a piece of broiled fish. When He swallowed it, and they watched it disappear, they knew He wasn't a mirage. He was the Son of Man, the Son of God, their long-awaited Messiah, and their bona fide leader in flesh once again.

What Jesus had shown them was the difference between a glorified body and no body. He was real and tangible, but He didn't have His former body or appearance. He could appear and disappear in the blink of an eye. He could pass through solid objects, like grave clothes and walls, and He could travel long distances in seconds. He had a spiritual body suited for heaven.

The disciples were no longer frightened by Jesus or the Jewish authorities. They were bolstered by His presence, and their basic knowledge of ancient prophecies gave them a renewed sense of inner peace and patience. They knew God had promised to cast out their enemies and set up their Messiah as King of Israel. They wouldn't see disaster ever again, because the Lord their God would live with them in their midst (Zephaniah 3:14–20). They thought Jesus was finally going to rescue them from the Romans and reestablish Jerusalem as the honor of the earth, high above the other nations (Deuteronomy 26:19). They swung from being brokenhearted, confused, lost, and miserable to being immensely relieved and completely overjoyed. They wholeheartedly welcomed back their leader.

A week later, Jesus appeared to the disciples again in the same house. This time, Thomas was present (John 20:26). Since Thomas had not believed the other disciples when they told him they had seen the Lord, Jesus told Thomas to "stop doubting and believe." Then He invited Thomas to touch the marks on His hands and side (John 20:27).

Thomas did just that and then exclaimed in total reverence, "My Lord and my God!" (John 20:28).

The next time Jesus appeared to some of His disciples was early in the morning on the shore of Lake Galilee, also known as the Sea of Tiberias. Seven of them had been fishing all night. Jesus stood on the shore and called out to find out what they caught. The disciples did not recognize Him but answered that they had not caught anything. Jesus then instructed them, "Throw your net on the right side of the boat and you will find some" (John 21:6). When they complied, they caught more fish than they could haul into their boat. John told Peter, "It is the Lord!" (John 21:7), and they all returned immediately to meet Him onshore.

In the short time it took to get to shore, Jesus had created breakfast for them, much like the food He had created for the multitudes! He offered them fish cooked over coals and bread to go with it. He was still taking care of His disciples' needs.

After eating, Jesus asked Simon Peter three times if he loved Him. Each time Peter answered affirmatively. The first two times, Jesus used the word *agapaō,* meaning "a love of commitment." Peter could not respond using agapaō, because he had denied knowing Jesus three times on the night before He was crucified. Instead, he responded with the word *phileo,* indicating a love of strong emotion for Jesus. The third time, Jesus also used the word "phileo." Peter was saddened that Jesus came down to his level in using his word of warmth, fondness, and friendship. He adored Jesus, but he had not been able to make a full commitment. Nevertheless, Peter responded, "Lord, you know all things; you know that I love you" (John 21:17).

Yes, Jesus knew all things. He knew Peter's heart. He also knew that even though Peter had denied Him three times before the cock crowed, he had never lost faith in Him. Consequently, Jesus restored his fellowship, and put Peter back into service. He told Peter that if he loved Him, then he would "Feed my lambs" (John 21:15), "Take care of my sheep" (John 21:16), and, "Feed my sheep" (John 21:17). "Feed" conveyed nourishment through teaching and guiding. Feed them with what? With the Word of God! Jesus had drawn a commitment from Peter, after all. He had also assured the other disciples that He had completely forgiven Peter.

After reinstating Peter as an undershepherd in caring for His flock, Jesus made an appearance to more than five hundred believers in one gathering (1 Corinthians 15:6). This appearance was probably in Galilee, because that's where He told His disciples to meet Him, and that's where He had the most followers.

After preaching to the crowd, He appeared to James (the half-brother of Jesus) and then met His disciples again in Jerusalem for the last time. He told them not to leave Jerusalem. They were to wait for the gift of the Holy Spirit, promised by God the Father (Luke 24:49a). They would then be "clothed with power from on high" (Luke 24:49b), and "baptized with the Holy Spirit" (Acts 1:5).

The disciples were excited. They had no idea they would never see Jesus again, but they were eager to know why they were going to be "clothed with power." What was Jesus planning to do? Was He going to gather His armies to defeat the Romans? With great anticipation, they finally asked Him what they had really wanted to know since His resurrection: "Lord, are you at this time going to restore the kingdom to Israel?" (Acts 1:6).

Jesus did not consider their question to be foolish, but He did not answer it directly. He wasn't about to correct their hopeful vision. He merely corrected the timing of it, replying, "It is not for you to know the times or dates the Father has set up by His own authority. But you will receive power when the Holy Spirit comes on you; and you will be my witnesses in Jerusalem, and in all Judea and Samaria, and to the ends of the earth" (Acts 1:8).

After saying that, Jesus led His disciples outside toward Bethany. He lifted His hands to bless them and was taken up to heaven in a cloud of glory, right before their eyes (Luke 24:51, 52; Acts 1:2).

While the astonished disciples gazed into the sky after Him, two angels appeared and gave them an important message. They said, "Men of Galilee, why do you stand here looking into the sky? This same Jesus, who has been taken from you into heaven, will come back in the same way you have seen Him go into heaven" (Acts 1:11).

Knowing Jesus was still alive and coming back again in a cloud of power and glory, the disciples returned to Jerusalem with great joy. They stayed at the temple and praised God (Luke 24:52, 53). They waited there as instructed for Jesus to send the promised Spirit.

While waiting, they were absorbed in countless discussions of all the recent events in relation to their ancient prophecies. Jesus had opened their minds (Luke 24:45), just as He had opened the minds of the two believers on the road to Emmaus (Luke 24:27). Suddenly, the disciples understood His life in light of its spiritual significance. Everything He had said and done was beginning to make beautiful sense.

Jesus had not come to earth to save anyone from the Romans. He had come to save *everyone* from God's condemnation! Sin had separated all people from God, but God loved humankind so much that He sent His perfect Son to earth as the perfect sacrifice for all the sins of the world. Those who believed Jesus was the Son of God and came to die on the cross for their sins would not perish but live forever (John 3:16).

The pieces were clicking into place. Jesus was going to spread this good news to the entire world through them, His beloved disciples. They remembered how Jesus had told them over and over that He was going to be handed over to the authorities and suffer, die, and rise again in three days (Matthew 16:21–26; 17:22, 23; Mark 8:31–38; 9:30–32; Luke 9:22–25, 43–45).

They remembered what He had told them at supper on the night before He died. He said He was leaving to prepare a place in heaven for them. He said He would come back for them, so they could live with Him forever (John 14:1–3).

They remembered His death, resurrection, ascension—and what the two angels had just told them. Jesus had been taken to heaven, but He was alive and coming back again. A second coming. No wonder they had been so confused!

They remembered He told them He would always be with them, "to the end of the age" (Matthew 28:20). What age? The age of the Holy Spirit … His Spirit. The age of the church … His church, His believers.

They remembered His words, "I will build my Church" (Matthew 16:18), and, "You will be my witnesses" (Acts 1:8).

They realized Jesus was going to send them out as His apostles and spokesmen for the third time. (See Matthew 10, Mark 6:7–13, and Luke 9:1–6 for details of their first two missions.) Jesus was going to empower them again with His Spirit. The next time, they would be enabled to teach people about His kingdom to come. They would be able to preach His messages and heal the sick. Even more important, they would be able to link His death, resurrection, and ascension to their Jewish Scriptures. This time, with more signs and wonders in His name, they would be able to prove Jesus was very much alive and living through them! The kingdom of God had not died on the cross.

The disciples finally realized that very few of their religious leaders would ever accept Jesus' authority over them. He really had been a direct threat to their hierarchies and futures as the people's choice of leadership. But He had never been a threat to the commoners. He sided with the minions. And now through His apostles, He was going to reach the multitudes. They were going to be the ones who to spread His good news and promises to the ends of the earth. Bring Him on!

What is this "good news"? It's the assurance that none of them would perish. No one has to perish. Even though all humans deserve to go straight to a hell separate from God, Jesus provided a way out.

Everyone now has the option of living for God or living for self, as long as His messages circulate … as long as His church and His Holy Spirit remain in this world.

The disciples realized Jesus had returned to His former place at the right hand of God the Father Almighty, but His Spirit would always live in the hearts of everyone who believes in Him. Their new job would be to open more hearts.

# 41
## Empowerment of the Holy Spirit

The enlightened disciples didn't have long to wait. The Holy Spirit arrived on the day of Pentecost, ten days after Jesus' ascension. "Pentecost" is derived from the Greek word meaning "fifty." It occurred fifty days after Passover. It was also called the day of firstfruits (Exodus 23:16), because the Israelites were supposed to bring the best examples of their first crops harvested each year and dedicate them to God, thereby acknowledging all things come from and belong to Him. In turn for their obedience, God promised prosperity to those who honored Him with their firstfruits (Proverbs 3:10).

Though Pentecost was a feast of joy and thanksgiving for the end of the harvest season, it was primarily a reminder that the land of Canaan was not their land. It was God's possession, and they were merely His tenants (Leviticus 25:23). Furthermore, its fertility and their prosperity were His gifts, not the gifts of lesser gods.

It was no coincidence that the Holy Spirit arrived on the day of Pentecost. It was fifty days after Jesus died, and He was described as "the firstfruits of those who have fallen asleep" (1 Corinthians 15:20). Also, Pentecost was the second of three major Jewish religious holidays. Attendance before God in the temple was required of all Jewish men (Exodus 34:23, 24), so Jerusalem was brimming once again with Jewish visitors from many Mediterranean nations who didn't speak Hebrew or Aramaic. What an opportune time for God to unite all of them with a stunning audiovisual display and an extraordinary miracle!

On the day of Pentecost, the chosen disciples were all in one place (Acts 2:1). Thousands of people were milling about in the streets of Jerusalem, but Jesus' disciples stayed together and waited for what their Master had promised.

His promise happened suddenly. With a sound *like* a violent wind and a sight *like* tongues of fire, separating and settling on each of the eleven disciples, they were, "filled with the Holy Spirit," and began

*Lee Merrick*

to speak in other tongues or foreign languages, "as the Spirit enabled them" (Acts 2:4).

There wasn't any real fire. Much like the burning bush in Exodus 3:2–6, the tongues of fire didn't burn anything. There wasn't any wind, either, but there was a noise like that of freight trains. The flames and wind were supernatural indicators of God's holiness and presence. In ancient Scripture, fire and wind were frequently symbolic of divine presence (e.g., Exodus 13:21, 22; 24:17; Job 38:1; Ezekiel 1:4).

The noise brought Jerusalem residents and Jewish foreigners together to see the sound and light show. As they arrived, they were astonished to hear the disciples declare the wonders of God in foreign languages and distinctive dialects. How in the world were uneducated, uncultured Galileans able to do that?

Some made fun of the disciples by suggesting they were drunk. Others knew they were not drunks, but the question remained, "What does this mean?" (Acts 2:12).

Peter was the one who stood up and explained that what they heard was Jewish prophecy being fulfilled. Empowered by the Holy Spirit to present the gospel truth to the people, Peter was the first disciple who linked Jewish Scripture to the life, death, and resurrection of Jesus. Quoting God's prophet Joel, Peter bravely stated that God warned the people what He was going to do in the last days of the age. He said, "I will pour out my Spirit on all people ... I will show signs on earth below ... before the coming of the great and glorious day of the LORD. And anyone who calls on the name of the LORD will be saved" (Joel 2:28–32). Then Peter continued, convincing the crowd that Jesus really was their Messiah. He said, "Jesus of Nazareth was a man accredited by God to you by miracles, wonders and signs which God did among you through Him ... This man was handed over to you by God's set purpose and foreknowledge ... and you put Him to death by nailing Him to a cross. But God raised Him from the agony of death because it was impossible for death to keep its hold on Him" (Acts 2:22–24).

166

Then Peter turned the screw a little more, saying, "God has raised this Jesus to life, and we are all witnesses. Exalted to the right hand of God, Jesus has received from the Father the promised Holy Spirit, and has poured out what you now see and hear ... Therefore, let all Israel be assured of this: God has made this Jesus, whom you crucified, both Lord and Christ" (Acts 2:32–36).

When the people heard Peter's explanation, they were "cut to the heart" (Acts 2:37). They believed him and were stunned and sorrowfully distressed over his accusation. Lord have mercy, they had killed their Messiah! In sincere remorse, they asked Peter what they could do to save themselves from condemnation. Peter replied, "Repent and be baptized, every one of you, in the name of Jesus Christ for the forgiveness of your sins. And you will receive the gift of the Holy Spirit" (Acts 2:38).

Repentance and baptism were, and are, the keys to forgiveness. Repentance is far more demanding than merely regretting a sin and wanting to escape from the consequences of God's judgment. It is more than an academic change of mind or a flat acceptance of the Person and Word of God. It is a radical turning from God's views of wrong to God's views of right.

Repentance will not make you righteous overnight. It will gradually change your lifestyle and become manifest by the fruits of the Holy Spirit, which are love, joy, peace, patience, kindness, goodness, faithfulness, gentleness, and self-control (Galatians 5:22). These desirable attributes are God-given. They are not badges of merit people can earn. God knows our hearts. If they are sincere and we truly desire to live our lives for Him instead of merely for ourselves, He will forgive our sins, baptize us with the Holy Spirit, and help us become the person He created us to be.

This spiritual baptism is a one-time act of God. The believer in Jesus Christ is indwelt by the Spirit of God, sealed in faith until Jesus comes again, and placed into His church, the spiritual body of Christ. God is the only One who can seal our salvation, because He is the only One who truly knows our hearts.

The water baptism after repentance was the believer's public confession of faith in Jesus Christ as Lord and Savior. It was an outward sign of an inner faith, and an identification with Jesus. It was also a dangerous move, because it didn't win any favor in the eyes of the religious officials who remained in opposition to Jesus.

Peter's message went out to the "men of Israel" (Acts 2:22). Every one of them were "God-fearing Jews from every nation under heaven" (Acts 2:5). About three thousand of them accepted his message and were baptized that day (Acts 2:41). The Christian church was born on the day of Pentecost, and it was 100 percent Jewish!

The specific number listed in Scripture suggests that records of baptism were kept. Archaeology today supports the possibility of so many ancient baptisms in one day. Numerous Jewish *mikvahs* have been uncovered on the southern side of the Temple Mount. These mikvahs were large facilities where worshippers purified themselves by a full immersion in water before entering the temple. They certainly could have been used for more than one purpose.

# 42
## Power and Joy

There was a tremendous difference in the apostles between Passover and Pentecost. During Passover, after Jesus was arrested, the disciples ran for their lives. They were terrified that the religious leaders would have them arrested, also. Peter denied knowing Jesus three times, and John was the only disciple who stood at the foot of His cross. All the rest cowered in their hiding places.

When Jesus showed up after His death and burial, most of the disciples thought He was a ghost, which moved them into a different stage of disbelief and fear. Understanding their discomposure, Jesus stayed with them for forty days and presented Himself to over five hundred witnesses, who had been chosen by God (Acts 10:41). His appearances changed the wild rumors of His resurrection into convincing proof that He was not a ghost (Acts 1:3). He was not only alive, but He was with them in person and still preaching about His kingdom to come. He completely restored their faith in Him.

During His earthly ministry with them, the disciples had expected Him to establish His kingdom on earth, but it had not happened. When He came back to them, they thought it would happen soon, but it didn't. Then when He ascended into heaven, shortly after telling Peter to feed His sheep and telling all of them to take His messages to the end of the earth, they realized He had thrown His mission into their hands. Ten days later, when He empowered them with His Spirit on the day of Pentecost, they knew exactly what they were to do with it.

Emboldened with a new sense of power, the apostles hit the streets in a brave, new style. They were on a new spiritual high! None of them ever considered again that Jesus was gone from their midst. His ascension and their subsequent empowerment merely signified changes in the way He was going to continue His ministry.

Wherever the apostles went, they proclaimed that Jesus was the Son of God and the Messiah. They were not talking about a dead Messiah. They were talking about a living Messiah, who lived within them and walked beside them. They spoke the same words that got Him killed. Their fear of imprisonment or death had been erased. They had no doubt that He was who He always said He was, and they were willing to die for what they knew to be true.

The apostles' presentations were always powerful, because they had seen and heard it all. They had lived with Him for three years and were eyewitnesses to everything that happened from John's baptism, when the Spirit descended upon Jesus in the form of a dove, to the moment He had been taken from them into heaven. They had seen life after death, and their faith in Him was based on infallible proofs, not myths or speculation.

Their faces were radiant with exuberance, and their countenance was changed. Their uninhibited enthusiasm was contagious. Three thousand people signed up with them the first day! An infant church had taken root, and a revolution was under way, a revolution without any weapons. A revolution powered by God the Father, God the Son, and God the Holy Spirit through the hearts of simple men who knew Whom they were serving.

The new believers were also jubilant. They enjoyed their new fellowship with Jesus and the other believers. They never rejected their strong Jewish faith in one God, or their customs or religious holidays, but they saw Jesus Christ as the fulfillment of everything they had learned in their synagogues. They had failed to realize He was their Messiah when He came to earth the first time as a humble servant, because they had been led astray. But now they knew He was coming back as Lord of Lords, and they were watching for His glorious return, as instructed (Matthew 24:42; 25:13; Mark 13:34–37).

These first converts did not speak in tongues, but they were gifted with a hunger to learn God's will and the courage to walk in His ways. They, "devoted themselves to the apostles' teaching" (Acts 2:42), so their spiritual foundation continued to grow and mature. They met each other every day in the temple (Acts 2:46), where they praised God the Father for sending His Son to them, and they thanked Jesus for what He had done for them. They continued to observe their three hours of daily prayer (9 a.m., noon, and 3 p.m.). And they also broke bread in their homes in new observance of the Lord's Table and His communion with His saints.

They gradually learned which rules were binding and which were not. As they unharnessed themselves from the trivial and extremely restrictive oral laws, their daily lives became less burdensome. They began to live happy, simple lives based on Christ instead of on the Pharisees. They were no longer enticed by money, possessions, power, or popularity. They did not covet. They were not jealous of anyone. They gladly shared what they had with other believers. They did not live in a commune or redistribute everything equally, but they readily sold their possessions to provide money for those in their church who were in need (Acts 2:44, 45).

The new believers were very secure in the realm of God's blessings, and they welcomed all new believers. They never considered their growing church to be an exclusive entity for saints. On the contrary, they considered it to be an inclusive entity for fellow sinners and were ever joyful, because they knew that all forgiven sinners would be going to heaven.

Genuine conversions did not always lead to extraordinary signs, wonders, or miracles. But they always enabled new believers to speak out about Christ and spread the story of His provisions for the world through His life, death, and resurrection. That's why the new believers were able to witness to the gospel in the temple courts (Acts 5:42).

Supernatural things always authenticated the apostles and their associates as special messengers of God. The apostles were generally the ones who were empowered to speak in tongues. Occasionally, they passed it along to others (Acts 10:44–48; 19:1–7). The apostles and their close associates (Stephen, Paul, and Barnabas) performed the miracles, signs, and wonders after the ascension.

# 43
## Warnings

Not long after the three thousand believers converted, thousands more were reassured of the new faith based on infallible facts. They repented also, and the church in Jerusalem quickly grew to five thousand (Acts 4:4).

At first, the Romans and the Jewish religious leaders were merely annoyed with the zesty apostles and new recruits. They expected the new Jesus frenzy to die down, but it didn't. It continued to grow. Their edgy toleration ground to a halt when Peter and John healed a crippled beggar at the temple (Acts 3:7) and attributed his complete restoration and elation to his faith in Jesus (Acts 3:16).

Peter's pronouncement outraged the Sadducees, who did not believe in resurrection. Jolted into disciplinary action, the captain of the temple guard, some priests, and some Sadducees seized Peter and John and put them in jail for the night (Acts 4:3).

Before Jesus was crucified, His major opponents were the Pharisees. After He was crucified, the Pharisees backed down, and the Sadducees became the worst opponents of Christianity.

The Sadducees were rich descendants of the high priests who controlled the crooked and oppressive hierarchy of the temple. They supported the status quo and the ruling power of the Romans, so they were not well liked by the Jewish masses.

There was an enormous difference between the few materialistic high priests and the thousands of humble, regular priests. The humble priests were devoted men of God. Many of them realized, after the crucifixion, that Jesus was exactly who He said He was, and they became obedient to His new faith (Acts 6:7).

The day after Peter and John were thrown in jail, they were brought before the council of rulers, elders, and teachers of the law. The Sanhedrin council wanted to know by what power or name they had healed the cripple (Acts 4:7). Empowered by the Holy Spirit, Peter courageously replied, "Rulers and elders of the people! If we are being called to account today for an act of kindness shown to a cripple, and are asked how he was healed, then know this, you and all the people of Israel: It is by the name of Jesus Christ of Nazareth, whom you crucified but whom God raised from the dead, that this man stands before you healed" (Acts 4:8).

After his response, Peter, John, and the former cripple were asked to leave the room while the council discussed the matter. They were stymied, because everyone in Jerusalem knew that Peter and John had performed an outstanding miracle in the name of Jesus. They couldn't deny it, and they couldn't punish the apostles because the masses were praising God for what they had done. So to keep the peace yet keep the radical new faith from growing any larger, they decided to warn the apostles to stop speaking publicly in the name of Jesus (Acts 4:15–17).

When they summoned the apostles and issued their supreme warning, Peter and John replied, "Judge for yourselves whether it is right in God's sight to obey you rather than God. For we cannot help speaking about what we have seen and heard" (Acts 4:19,20).

The Sanhedrin could do nothing more, so they issued further threats and let them go. Peter and John returned to their own people and reported everything that was said. The people prayed to God to elicit His response: "Now, Lord, consider their threats and enable your servants to speak your word with great boldness. Stretch out your hand to heal and perform miraculous signs and wonders through the name of your holy servant Jesus" (Acts 4:29,30).

Their prayers were answered immediately! The place where they were meeting was shaken. They were all filled with the Holy Spirit, and they continued to speak the Word of God boldly (Acts 4:31).

Being "filled with the Holy Spirit" was repetitive and not the same thing as the one-time-only baptism by the Holy Spirit, which sealed and protected believers until the Second Coming. The gifts of the Holy Spirit were distributed randomly, according to God's will. Different people were filled with different spiritual gifts. Some were repeated. Some were not. God knew believers would face more and more opposition as they spread the gospel throughout the world, so He gave them new powers as they needed them.

# 44
## Persecution

The vehement opposition to the spread of Christianity began as the apostles started performing miracles in Jesus' name (Acts 5:12). People started bringing their sick friends and acquaintances into the streets. They laid them on beds and mats so that they might be healed by an apostle's shadow as he walked by (Acts 5:15). Word spread, and more people brought the sick and handicapped from towns all around Jerusalem. All of them were healed (Acts 5:16).

The high priest and all of his associates, who were Sadducees, felt threatened again by the immense power of the apostles. The Jewish people were beginning to support the miracle workers, who were challenging their disbeliefs of resurrection and life after death. Worse yet, the people agreed with the charges of the apostles that the religious authorities had murdered the Messiah. Consequently, a group of Sadducees arrested the apostles and threw them back in the public jail.

That night, an angel of the Lord unlocked the doors of the jail and took the apostles outside. He instructed them to go to the temple courts the next morning and tell the people, "the full message of this new life" (Acts 5:20). The apostles did as they were told.

The next morning, the high priest called the Sanhedrin together and ordered the apostles to appear before the full council. The officers went to get the apostles and found the guards standing at the doors but no apostles in jail. Someone informed the council that the apostles were all teaching in the courtyards of the temple, so guards were sent there to bring them back to appear before the political and religious rulers.

The high priests reminded the apostles that they had been given strict orders not to teach anymore in the name of Jesus Christ. The apostles quickly responded to the priests, "Yet you have filled Jerusalem with your teaching, and are determined to make us guilty of this man's blood" (Acts 5:28). Peter bravely supported the other apostles and told the high priests, "We must obey God rather than men! The God of our fathers raised Jesus from the dead—whom you had killed by hanging on a tree. God exalted him to his own right hand as Prince and Savior that he might give repentance and forgiveness of sins to Israel. We are witnesses of these things, and so is the Holy Spirit, whom God has given to those who obey him" (Acts 5:29–32).

The council members were livid over the continued accusations. They wanted to put all of them to death. But a highly respected rabbi and Pharisee named Gamaliel stood up on their behalf. He ordered someone to take the apostles outside the room for a while, so the council could resume their discussion in private.

When the apostles left, Gamaliel advised the Sanhedrin to "Leave these men alone! Let them go! For if their purpose or activity is of human origin, it will fail. But if it is from God, you will not be able to stop these men; you will only find yourselves fighting against God" (Acts 5:38,39).

Gamaliel's brilliant speech persuaded the Sanhedrin not to kill the apostles. They were not executed, but they were flogged. After the cruel lashings, they were ordered not to speak in the name of Jesus again and finally released.

Amazingly, the apostles never complained about their treatment or felt sorry for themselves. Being filled with the Holy Spirit, they actually rejoiced that God had used them to extend His kingdom (Acts 5:41). This was the first incidence of physical persecution against the new church, and the positive responses of the tortured apostles set a precedent for future believers who would also be persecuted.

In brave defiance of ruling orders, the apostles continued to preach the good news that the Messiah had come and gone but still ruled through the Spirit of Jesus.

Persecution turned deadly when some local Jewish residents picked on a Jewish outsider named Stephen, who was a young leader in the new church. Stephen was full of God's loving kindness and power, so he was a very popular young leader. He performed great wonders and miracles for the people (Acts 6:8). But he had not been born in Palestine, so he was considered a second-class citizen by many of the local Jews, who had been born in Jerusalem.

These local residents didn't like watching Stephen rise higher in their new church than he could have risen in their community, so they opposed his emergence as a prominent new leader. Much to their chagrin, though, they were not able to stand up against Stephen's knowledge of Scripture or his power of public speaking. So they resorted to deceit and conspiracy. They persuaded false witnesses to spread lies about him (Acts 6:11). This conspiracy was similar to what the chief priests and Sanhedrin did when they had used false evidence against Jesus to put Him to death (Matthew 26:59–61).

The lies worked. They stirred up the people by convincing them Stephen was attacking the very things they held most sacred—their temple, their Jewish law, Moses, and even God. In retaliation, some elders and teachers of the law seized Stephen and brought him before their supreme court. They also summoned the false witnesses, who lied once again: "This fellow never stops speaking against the holy place and against the law ... We have heard him say that this Jesus of Nazareth will destroy this place and change the customs Moses handed down to us" (Acts 6:13, 14).

When the high priest asked Stephen if the charges were true, Stephen did not answer directly. Instead, with the face of an angel (Acts 6:15), he masterfully defended the new Christian faith by using old Jewish Scriptures. He gave a precise history of Israel and bravely compared the religious authorities' recent rejection of Jesus with their Jewish ancestors' rejection of God's prophets.

In conclusion, Stephen confronted his opponents with scathing words that led to his death. Accusing the leaders of treason and murder, he said, "You stiff-necked people with uncircumcised hearts and ears! You are just like your fathers: You always resist the Holy Spirit! Was there ever a prophet your fathers did not persecute? They even killed those who predicted the coming of the Righteous One. And now you have betrayed and murdered him. You have received the law that was put into effect through angels, but have not obeyed it" (Acts 7:51–53).

Stephen's accusations infuriated the leaders. They rushed over to him, dragged him out of the city, and stoned him to death (Acts 7:57,58). Their response was not a legal one. It was a flash mob reaction. They took Stephen outside the city walls, because Jewish law forbade executions within the Holy City. But Romans didn't allow Jewish people to inflict capital punishment at all, so stoning Stephen to death was a violation of Roman law.

Stephen's death sparked a tremendous persecution of new believers in Jerusalem, which was sanctioned by the high priests (Acts 22:5), and led by a young new leader of Christian opposition named Saul of Tarsus.

# 45
## Saint Paul

Saul was a Roman Jew. He was born in a Roman city called Tarsus, which is located in modern Turkey, just inland from the Mediterranean Sea. He was raised in Jerusalem but claimed Roman citizenship (Acts 22:3). His Hebrew name was Saul; his Roman name was Paulos (Paul). He was called both.

Saul grew up in a strict Jewish family that adhered to all the religious and cultural traditions (Acts 26:4, 5). He learned to read and write at an early age by copying passages of Scripture at his synagogue day school. He learned Hebrew and Aramaic as a small child and learned Greek a little later.

Sometime in his teens, Saul studied under the famous rabbi Gamaliel, who was the best Jewish teacher of that day (Acts 22:3). He became well versed in both Jewish Scripture and traditions (original written laws and added oral laws). As Saul said of himself, "I was advancing in Judaism beyond many Jews of my own age, and was extremely zealous for the traditions of my fathers" (Galatians 1:14). He worked very hard to learn and obey the stringent Sabbath and food laws. Eventually, he became a Pharisee (Acts 26:5; Philippians 3:5).

"Advancing in Judaism" put Saul at odds with Jesus, because Judaism was a religious system of self-achievement. It was a life of working to please God and to gain righteousness in His eyes. Jesus knew that righteousness was God-given and not something that could be earned. Judaism was not based on the written laws of God found in Genesis, Exodus, Leviticus, Numbers, and Deuteronomy. It was based on the *oral* traditions, which the rabbis gradually made to be as binding as the written laws. Jesus never accepted the trivial oral laws, so Saul never accepted Jesus as an authority during His earthly ministry.

Before Jesus started His ministry, most Jews did not study the Jewish Scriptures. They knew a little about their history from religious holidays and festive customs, but they only received a limited religious education from rabbinic interpretations of Scripture.

Jesus objected to what they were taught. Some of the oral laws were not in Scripture at all, and some of them actually contradicted it (Mark 7:13). Jesus wanted the people to learn the divine implications of God's laws instead of the human interpretations of the rabbis. He died trying to teach God's original intentions to His chosen people.

The Jews against Jesus did not believe He was their Messiah, so they never referred to His followers as "Christians"; Christ was the title for Messiah. They disdainfully called them Nazarenes. Saul was no exception. He considered all Nazarenes to be obstacles of the advancement of Judaism, so he pursued them in Jerusalem and tried to destroy the church (Galatians 1:13, 14). He approved of Stephen's execution and took an active part in it. He not only watched him die, he guarded the clothes of those who were throwing the stones (Acts 22:20).

Saul's violent campaigns were all sanctioned by the Sanhedrin, which was the puppet supreme court of Israel. Paul got permission from the high priests to arrest the new believers and put them in prison. When they were put to death, his votes were recorded against them as Nazarenes who identified with Jesus as their primary religious authority (Acts 26:10). He went from one synagogue to another to have them punished, and he tried to force them to blaspheme (Acts 26:11).

Stephen's death and Saul's rampant persecution caused many new believers to leave town. The apostles stayed in Jerusalem to care for the victims and continue their evangelism, but many residents scattered into neighboring provinces (Acts 8:1).

Opponents of Jesus thought their strategy to kill Stephan was brilliant, because the subsequent persecution was snowballing, and the new wayward church couldn't possibly survive. But they were wrong. Their strategy failed, because the scattered believers became missionaries as well as refugees. They preached God's Word wherever they went (Acts 8:4). Christianity spread out of Jerusalem to all Judea and Samaria, just as Jesus knew it would (Acts 1:8). The blood of martyrs really was the "seed of the church". (Father Tertullian: www.reformationtheology.com/2006/05/the_blood_of_the_martyrs.

php) As the new believers scattered, Saul chased after them like a bounty hunter. In his obsession against them, he went to foreign cities with letters of permission from the high priest and the council to haul them back to Jerusalem to be punished (Acts 22:5; 26:11). His persecutions came to a sudden halt, though, when he met Jesus on the road to Damascus.

As Saul approached Damascus, he was blinded by an intense flash of light from heaven. He fell to the ground and heard a voice ask, "Saul, Saul, why do you persecute me?" (Acts 9:4; 22:6; 26:14). When Saul asked who was speaking, Jesus answered, "I am Jesus, whom you are persecuting ... Now get up and go into the city, and you will be told what you must do" (Acts 9:5, 6).

The men traveling with Saul saw the light and heard the voice. But they couldn't understand what was said, because it was spoken in Arabic (Acts 26:14). They led the now-blind Saul into the city. He remained blind for three days (Acts 9:9).

Jesus sent a disciple in Damascus named Ananias to place his hands on Saul so that his eyes would be healed, and he would be filled with the Holy Spirit. Ananias was also instructed to tell Saul God chose him to be an apostle to the Gentiles. Saul was to carry His name before the people of Israel and before the Gentiles and their kings (Acts 9:15).

When Saul regained his eyesight, Ananias told him God had chosen him to know His will, see Him in person, and hear the words from His mouth (Acts 22:14). First, though, Saul had to be baptized to wash away his sins and enable him to call on the name of the Lord (Acts 22:16).

When Saul called on His name, Jesus appeared and said, "I am Jesus, whom you are prosecuting ... I have appeared to you to appoint you as a servant and as a witness of what you have seen of me, and what I will show you. I will rescue you from your own people and from the Gentiles. I am sending you to them to open their eyes and turn them from darkness to light, and from the power of Satan to the power of God, so that they may receive forgiveness of sins and a place among those who are sanctified by faith in me" (Acts 26:15–18).

Saul never wavered or wondered. He had seen God's revelation through a blinding light, through a man named Ananias, and now through His Son in person! Saul responded to this second awesome encounter with Jesus by turning to Him in faith and commitment. He didn't stay in Damascus to discuss anything further with Ananias. Nor did he race back to Jerusalem to ask the apostles to clarify his astounding revelations. He had seen and heard enough. Filled with the Holy Spirit, he headed southeast immediately and went into the Nabatean desert area of Arabia, where he received further instructions and enlightenment from the Lord (Galatians 1:17). As he wrote later in his New Testament epistles, "The gospel I preached is not something that man made up. I did not receive it from any man, nor was I taught it; rather, I received it from revelation from Jesus Christ" (Galatians 1:11).

Saul was homeschooled in the wilderness by the Lord. He learned who Jesus was, why He came to earth the first time, what He had provided for the world through His death on the cross, what He expected from new believers, what God's overall plan was for humanity, and how he was going to fit into God's plan as an apostle to the Gentiles. Saul felt he had been turned inside out. Jesus had intervened in his life to teach him that he wasn't going to get to heaven by trusting in his own efforts to keep the stringent Jewish laws, because God's righteousness cannot be earned. He was going to get to heaven by trusting in Jesus, because righteousness is freely given through God's loving kindness to everyone who believes in His Son (Galatians 2:16). The traditional oral laws were certainly important, but they weren't the be-all or end-all. The old system of legalism had been put in charge just long enough to lead people to Christ (Galatians 3:24), and Saul was ready to lead.

Saul was a highly educated Pharisee who knew all the Old Testament laws. He also knew that all prophecies in Scripture pointed to the coming Messiah. The problem was that he had never accepted Jesus as his Lord and Savior, so he had never accepted the authority of His messages or attempted to apply them to his life.

All things had changed for Saul on that road to Damascus. He suddenly realized that all the ancient prophecies pointed directly to Jesus, so the former controlling power of his life had changed completely. As he said later in his epistles, "I died to the law so that I might live for God" (Galatians 2:19). Saul became anxious and driven to introduce the enlightening truth to the world. Jesus set him free from the supervision of Judaism and empowered him to set others free. Saul was ready, willing, and enabled.

Fully informed and forever thankful, Saul returned to Gentile Damascus and began preaching the gospel in the synagogues (Galatians 1:17). The people there were skeptical and stunned. They remembered him as a fiery prosecutor of the new believers, not someone who would ever defend their radical new faith. His former peers, who had never accepted Jesus as the Messiah, were infuriated with his messages. They conspired to kill him (Acts 9:23), but his new followers helped him escape.

Saul returned to Jerusalem and stayed with Peter for fifteen days (Galatians 1:18). Peter was the most powerful spokesman in the Jerusalem church in the early years, and Saul wanted to discuss the gospel with him. Saul didn't see any of the other apostles except James, the half-brother of Jesus, but he saw many of the new believers. They were still afraid of him. They remembered his brutal campaign against them and had a hard time believing he was really on their side (Acts 9:26).

Barnabas came to vouch for Saul. Barnabas was an encouraging fellow Jew, who convinced them that Saul had actually seen the resurrected Lord and had preached as fearlessly in His name in Damascus as he had spoken against Him in Jerusalem (Acts 9:27). Saul gained their confidence, but he irritated the Greek-speaking Jews who had opposed Stephen. They tried to kill him, also (Acts 9:29).

Once again, Saul's brothers in faith came to his rescue. They took him to Caesarea and sent him off to Tarsus (Acts 9:30). Caesarea was a seaport and the capital city of the Roman province of Judea. Tarsus was Saul's birthplace and a key city of trade in the Roman province of Cilicia.

After Saul left Jerusalem, the apostles there received wonderful news that many of the new believers who had fled from Jerusalem after Stephen's death had gone to Antioch of Syria and established a large, mixed congregation of new believers there. The church of Jerusalem sent Barnabas to Antioch to verify the reports.

Antioch of Syria was the third-largest city in the Roman Empire, behind Rome and Alexandria. It was home to many Jews who had been raised outside of Palestine. They lived among Greek Gentiles who worshipped multiple gods, but the Antioch Jews kept their faith in their one almighty God. Some spoke Hebrew. Most spoke Greek. They were called Diaspora Jews, and the new believers from Jerusalem had fled to them.

When the refugees arrived in Antioch of Syria, they shared the good news about Jesus in both Hebrew and Greek. The Lord's hand was with them, and a great number of people there became followers of the Lord (Acts 11:19–21).

Barnabas quickly confirmed the reports and stayed there to help them. He was an ideal missionary for the large, mixed congregation, because he was a Greek-speaking Roman Jew from Cyprus, He had a cultural background very similar to that of most of the residents in Antioch.

Barnabas loved his mission, but he needed help. Antioch was too large for him to teach and encourage the people effectively by himself, so he went to Tarsus and searched for Saul. He found him, and readily noticed that he had gone back to using his given Roman name of Paul. He asked Paul to return to Antioch with him. Paul obliged.

Barnabas and Paul worked together for a year and were very successful. Antioch of Syria became known as the first Gentile church, and their student disciples were the first followers of Christ to be called Christians (Acts 11:26). Christianity was no longer a small sect of Nazarenes. It was very much an offshoot of Judaism, but it was becoming something far more than just a Jewish thing.

While Paul and Barnabas were still there, God sent some prophets to Antioch. One of them, Agabus, announced that a severe famine was going to spread over the entire Roman Empire (Acts 11:27). The disciples in Antioch collected money for their brothers in Judea and sent it to them with Paul and Barnabas. They always took care of their home church.

From Jerusalem, in AD 47, Paul set out on his first of three well-known missionary journeys. He traveled with Barnabas for two more years. They focused on spreading more Gentile churches in the Roman Empire. Peter stayed in one area and focused on spreading more Jewish churches in Jerusalem and Judea.

Peter and James spread the message to the new churches in Judea that "the man who formerly prosecuted us is now preaching the faith he once tried to destroy" (Galatians 1:23), and all the Judeans praised God for Paul.

Whenever Paul entered a new city, he preached to the Jews first. If he had preached to the Gentiles first, the Jews wouldn't have listened to him. His Roman citizenship, his studies under Gamaliel, and his status as a former Pharisee in Jerusalem gave him the respect he needed to attract substantial crowds of Roman Jews. He usually began his sermons at a synagogue on the Sabbath (Acts 13:14; 14:1; 17:1,10,17; 18:4,19,26; 19:8). He would sit through the readings from the Law and the prophets and wait for the leaders to invite him to speak. They usually said something like, "Brothers, if you have a message of encouragement for the people, please speak" (Acts 13:15).

Knowing there would always be some Greek Gentiles at the Sabbath services, Paul often began his introduction with: "Men of Israel, and you Gentiles who worship God, listen to me" (Acts 13:16). Then he would launch into a brief history of the Israelites and their failure to recognize Jesus as their Messiah, or the kingdom of God, or what Jesus provided for the world by dying on the cross.

The Greek Gentiles who came to the Sabbath services leaned toward Judaism, because they leaned toward the almighty God of Israel, who created and ruled everything. They had heard all the amazing stories about His victories through faithful Israelites, so they came to worship Him and learn more about the miracle worker from Galilee who claimed to be His Son! Most of them became

God-fearing, but few of them adopted Jewish customs or went through the ritual of circumcision. They didn't have to, because they greatly outnumbered the Jews in most Roman provinces outside of Judea. The sandal was actually on the other foot. Many Jewish refugees adopted Greek customs. The Jews retained their faith but learned the Greek language and enjoyed their ways of life.

Paul's messages were not always popular. He frequently caused division in the synagogues, not only between the followers and opponents of Jesus as Lord and Savior, but also between the Jewish followers themselves, who were willing to share Jesus with the Gentiles but unwilling to share His kingdom with them. In their eyes, the Jews were God's chosen people, so no one else would be eligible for salvation. Heaven would be open for circumcised, religious, Jewish males and no one else.

In Paul's eyes, though, the Gentiles were heirs to God's kingdom with Israel. Through the gospel, the Jews and Gentiles were all members of one body, and they would share all the promises of Jesus Christ with each other (Ephesians 3:6). The Gentiles loved Paul's visions, and so did the Jewish women. But most Jewish men stormed out when Paul started preaching about the salvation of the Gentiles.

The Jewish religious leaders saw this rift among the new believers, and tried to lure their men away from the promises of Christianity and back into the familiar legalism of Judaism. This rift opened into a public showdown in another town named Antioch, which was in the province of Pisidia in Asia Minor (modern Turkey). Paul was warmly received by the Greek Gentiles after a Sabbath service in Pisidian Antioch. They liked what they heard and asked him to return again the next Sabbath so their friends could also hear his messages. Paul obliged, and nearly the whole town gathered to hear the Word of the Lord on the following Sabbath.

The Jewish religious authorities outside of Israel were jealous of the crowds flocking to Paul and publicly rejected his gospel message (Acts 13:44,45). Paul and Barnabas boldly countered their opposition and declared, "We had to speak the word of God to you first. Since you reject it and do not consider yourselves worthy of eternal life, we now turn to the Gentiles" (Acts 13:46).

Paul turned away from the religious leaders, because they had condemned themselves by continually opposing Jesus. But he never turned away from his own Jewish people. He always maintained a deep love for them (Romans 9:1–5). Wanting to save them, he continued to start his gospel sermons with them in each new city on all his journeys. But he knew the thrust of his ministry would be to the Gentiles. He knew his calling. God was using him to spread His revelations to people whose hearts could open to Jesus, because their minds had not been poisoned against Him.

Paul spoke to the Jews first, because God offered His plan of salvation to the Jews first: "Repentance and forgiveness will be preached in His Name to all nations, beginning at Jerusalem" (Luke 24:47). Paul always hoped his fellow Jews would grasp that the story of the gospel is the power of God for the salvation of everyone who accepts His Son as Lord and Savior: "first for the Jew, then for the Gentile" (Romans 1:16).

Though God offered salvation to the Jews first, He never planned for it to be an exclusive blessing for the Jews only. He planned to bring salvation "to the ends of the earth" by making specific Jews be "a light for the Gentiles" (Isaiah 49:6). Paul knew he had been called to be part of that light, so every time the Jews rejected his gospel message, he turned to the Gentiles (Acts 18:6; 19:9), who believed his messages and supported the spread of Christianity.

Paul was the first Christian missionary to the Gentiles and founder of many Christian churches. But he was not an administrator; he was a persuader. He persuaded the Jews to keep the new faith in Jesus and not to revert to the "working" system of Judaism. He explained that Judaism focused on human achievements to please God and made it difficult for people, because it enslaved them to meaningless requirements. On the other hand, Christianity focused on God's achievements to please humans. It made life better for people, because they knew they were loved, forgiven, and empowered to love and forgive others. When Christians modeled their lives on

Jesus, they were happier, because God's truths set them free from false doctrines and oppression. They were free to live wondrous, powerful, Spirit-filled, joyous lives!

Paul knew that traditional Jews based their salvation on keeping rules for the sake of the rules. He had done the same thing when he was a Pharisee. After his conversion and homeschooling in the Nabatean desert area, however, Paul believed rules should be kept for the sake of civilized humanity ... for the sake of treating others the way we would like to be treated ... for the sake of loving others because God loved us first ... for the sake of forgiving others because God forgave us first.

Paul directed the spiritual growth of his churches by teaching everyone that their salvation was based on their belief in Christ as their Lord and Savior. Period! There was nothing they could do to make God love them more or love them less, because His love is unconditional. His love is not conditioned by how many rules they choose to obey.

It was a very difficult concept for Paul to teach, because human love is very conditional. God's love surpasses the limited understanding of humans, and He knows it. God doesn't expect us to understand His love for us, but He does expect us to accept the fact it is freely given and cannot be earned. It frees us from running around inside a wheel.

Over and over, Paul urged people to simply believe. Believe more, work less, and stop trying so hard to gain God's favor.

Paul's missions were anything but comfortable or safe. He was constantly on the move and in danger of rivers, bandits, Jews, Gentiles, and false brothers of faith (2 Corinthians 11:26). He frequently faced opposition and persecution. His adversaries stirred up confusion, hatred, and resentment in every region he entered. Residents often rioted when he visited cities, and angry mobs would chase him out of towns, accusing him of "causing trouble all over the world" (Acts 17:5,6).

Why such treatment? Because Paul was a successful Christian missionary, who established enthusiastic churches almost everywhere he went. Consequently, he provoked jealousy in most communities throughout the Roman Empire.

Why was Paul successful amid all the strife? Because God was "building His church" and taking it to the center of the first-century world through Paul. God encouraged him to continue speaking in His name (Acts 18:9–11; 20:7–12). He also accomplished extraordinary miracles through him, which convinced the crowds of His presence, power, and approval of Paul. "In this way, the word of the Lord spread widely and grew in power" (Acts 19:20).

In every city, the Holy Spirit warned Paul of prisons and hardships he was about to face (Acts 20:23). Paul was stoned (Acts 14:9), beaten with rods, flogged (Acts 26:22,23), and shipwrecked three times. His former Jewish peers sought to destroy him (Acts 9:23–29; 23:12–15). They judged against him for his Christian ministry and sentenced him five times to "forty-lashes-minus-one," which was the maximum punishment allowed under Jewish law (2 Corinthians 11:24).

Paul never knew what the next day was going to bring. But he was always sure of his ultimate destiny. As a brilliant scholar of Scripture, He knew God would counsel him, guide him, hold his right hand through all trials, and then lead him into glory (Psalm 73:23). His motto and philosophy was always, "To live is Christ, to die is gain" (Philippians 1:21).

After his three missionary trips and approximately ten years of life on the road, Paul made his fateful trip back to Jerusalem, despite being warned repeatedly that he would be arrested and beaten there. When Paul entered the temple in Jerusalem, he was recognized instantly and seized by local agitators. They aroused the whole crowd by shouting, "Men of Israel, help us! This is the man who teaches all men everywhere against our people and our law and this place … And besides, he has brought Greeks into the temple area and defiled this holy place" (Acts 21:28).

False rumors had been spreading that Paul was teaching Jews outside of Palestine that they didn't have to keep their Jewish laws. He was also accused of profaning their beloved temple by bringing a Gentile into the inner courts, which were only for Jewish men.

Gentiles were allowed to worship God in the outer court only, and signs were posted on the gatehouse that they would be put to death for entering an inner court. Out of respect for the Jewish religion, the Romans authorized the death sentence for this offense, even for their own Roman citizens.

When the agitators started shouting, people came running from everywhere. They seized Paul, dragged him away from the temple, and tried to beat him to death. When the Romans saw what was happening, they sent hundreds of soldiers into the violent mob to save Paul. Paul told the commander that he was a Roman Jew and asked if he could talk to the angry crowd to defend himself. The commander gave Paul permission, and Paul addressed the people in Aramaic to remind them he was not a Gentile but a Jew like themselves. When they heard him speak in their own language, they quieted and listened to what he had to say.

Paul did not blame them for beating him. As a former Pharisee, he understood their zeal for God. He told them he used to feel the same hatred against new believers and persecuted them to their death—until he met Jesus on the road to Damascus. As Paul eased into his testimony about how his encounter with the Lord had changed his life, the crowd was listening but growing edgy. When he told them how the Lord spoke to him personally three years later, telling him to leave Jerusalem immediately because Jewish leaders would not accept his testimony about Him, the crowd began to identify with those Jewish authorities and side against Paul. And when he told them God said, "Go, I will send you far away to the Gentiles" (Acts 22:21), the crowd erupted again.

The people were offended by Paul's implication that Gentiles would ever be on equal footing with them before God without becoming Jewish first. Coming to God directly by faith alone and not through circumcision, rituals, and cultural changes was a preposterous concept. They started shouting, "Rid the earth of him. He's not fit to live!" (Acts 22:22). When some of the people in the crowd started to tear off their clothes in a frenzied preparation to stone Paul to death for blasphemy, the Roman commander ordered the soldiers to take him back to the barracks under protective custody.

The next day, the commander released Paul and ordered the Sanhedrin to assemble so he could find out why the Jews had turned against one of their own. Standing before the Jewish Supreme Court, Paul knew that he would not receive a fair hearing, so he skillfully divided the Pharisees from the Sadducees by exploiting their religious differences. Paul said, "My brothers, I am a Pharisee, the son of a Pharisee. I stand on trial because of my hope in the resurrection of the dead" (Acts 23:6). Paul appealed to the Pharisees for support, because he knew their religious beliefs were closer to Christianity than those of the Sadducees, who didn't believe in resurrection, life after death, angels, or demons.

His appeal was very successful. Some of the Pharisees stood up in Paul's defense and said, "We find nothing wrong with this this man ... What if a spirit or an angel has spoken to him?" (Acts 23:9).

The ensuing mayhem between the two religious factions became so violent that the commander thought Paul was going to be torn to pieces. He ordered the troops to take him by force again and return him to the barracks.

The following night, the Lord encouraged Paul not to be afraid, because he was under His sovereign care. He told Paul, "Take courage! As you have testified about me in Jerusalem, so you must also testify in Rome" (Acts 23:11).

The next morning, more than forty Jews conspired to ambush Paul when he left the barracks. They vowed not to eat or drink anything until they killed him. Paul's nephew heard about the plan and informed the Roman commander. Determined to get him out of Jerusalem safely that night, the commander summoned two of his centurions and ordered them to get a horse for Paul and take him under heavy guard (two hundred soldiers, two hundred spearman, and seventy horseman) to Governor Felix in Caesarea, the Roman capital of Judea (Acts 23:23). There was no ambush that night.

Five days later, the high priest from Jerusalem went to Caesarea to press charges against Paul. He was accompanied by some elders and a lawyer. Felix listened to their accusations and Paul's self-defense with interest, but he failed to make a decision or come to any conclusion. Instead, he ordered a centurion to keep Paul under guard but allowed him some freedom and permitted his friends to take care of his needs.

Felix was shrewd and corrupt. He was hoping Paul would offer him a bribe in exchange for his freedom, so he kept him in Roman custody for two years. He sent for him frequently to talk to him (Acts 24:26), but Paul never offered Felix anything.

When Felix was replaced by Porcius Festus two years later, the controversy over Paul was still burning. Jewish leaders wanted Festus to send Paul back to Jerusalem. They were still hoping to ambush and kill him along the way (Acts 25:3). Paul knew he wouldn't be tried fairly in Jerusalem, so he used his Roman citizenship and insisted on a trial before the Romans, not the Jews. Festus tried to appease both sides and asked if Paul would be willing to go back to Jerusalem but to stand trial there before him, the Roman governor of Judea.

Paul knew he would not receive justice in a provincial court, either, so he refused to leave Caesarea. He told Festus, "I am now standing before Caesar's court, where I ought to be tried. I have not done any wrong to the Jews, as you yourself know very well know … I do not refuse to die, but if the charges brought against me by the Jews are not true, no one has the right to hand me over to them. I appeal to Caesar!" (Acts 25:10).

Every Roman citizen had the right to appeal to the emperor if he thought he was not going to receive a fair trial. If such an appeal was declared valid, the prisoner would be sent to Rome for disposition of his case.

Festus conferred with his council and then responded to Paul: "You have appealed to Caesar. To Caesar you will go" (Acts 25:12).

Paul's appeal was declared valid by King Herod Agrippa II, the last of the prominent New Testament Herods. He was the son of the Herod who killed the apostle James and imprisoned Peter. After Paul's hearing, King Agrippa II met privately with Governor Festus and agreed Paul was not guilty of any crime. He could have been set free if he had not appealed to Caesar (Acts 26:30–32) What the king didn't realize, though, was that Paul had used his Roman rights very effectively to his and God's advantage! His Christian "muscle" was going to travel to the heart and capital of the first-century world!

Paul was sent to Rome by ships. On the last leg of his voyage, his ship wrecked in a storm on the island of Malta, about sixty miles south of Sicily. Three months later, he finally arrived in Rome, in AD 58.

Paul was not sent to prison. He was allowed to rent a house and live under guard for two years. He welcomed everyone who came to visit without any interference. The Roman Empire did not turn anti-Christian until AD 64, so until then, he was allowed to preach about the kingdom of God and teach about the ministry and mission of Jesus Christ. He also wrote the books of Ephesians, Philippians, Colossians, and Philemon during this period of house arrest in Rome.

The book of Acts ends before Paul's trial before Caesar, so his fate was left undecided. But most scholars believe Paul was acquitted and released in AD 61, and he continued to travel and preach for three more years.

The book of Timothy tells us Paul was thrown in prison again in AD 64, when Emperor Nero began his savage persecution of Christians. Paul's subsequent request for his cloak and parchments (2 Timothy 4:13) indicated he was arrested and hauled away suddenly, without any notice.

Paul knew he had little chance of ever regaining his freedom again. He told Timothy, "I am already being poured out like a drink offering, and the time has come for my departure" (2 Timothy 4:6). Even though he anticipated his execution, Paul stayed calm and strong. His inner peace came from knowing he had kept his faith and was going "home" to live with his Lord and Savior (2 Timothy 4:7, 8,18).

Paul's execution was not mentioned in the Bible. But early church historians wrote that he was condemned by Nero and beheaded sometime between AD 65 and 67.

Paul did not introduce Christianity to Rome, but as the first missionary to the Gentiles, he strengthened its foothold there. He convinced the Romans that Jesus really was the way, the truth, and the life—and the only window through which the world could see God. Nobody was going to get to heaven through any of the Roman or Greek gods. Furthermore, Paul revealed that salvation is not an escape from this world, but it is God's relationship with this world through His Son. Paul preached that the Spirit of Jesus Christ lives in all believers and helps them become wise, powerful, and joyful.

We can thank Paul for his faith and his gritty perseverance in getting the full gospel to Rome, which was the educational, cultural, and social hub of the world in his day. The phrase, "All roads lead to Rome," was more than just a figure of speech. All great minds came together there to discuss precepts, concepts, and new ideas. Their conclusions and revelations were sent out in every direction on all the major trade routes. That is how the Christian faith catapulted from a small sect of Nazarenes—who had witnessed a death, resurrection, and ascension—to a worldwide phenomenon of "salvation is from the Jews" (John 4:22). Little hinges opened big doors, and out went the Word!

# 46
## Day of the Lord

Christianity continued to face opposition and persecution everywhere, but the world was not equipped to fight the will of God then. Or now! Everything from the beginning of creation to the end of this world as we know it was designed by God for God. It was designed for His glory and our possibility of living with Him in paradise forever.

God has not changed and neither has His plan for humanity. It continues to move forward, and we are very much a part of it. "Thy kingdom come, thy will be done, on earth as it is in heaven" (Matthew 6:10). We can either accept this truth or reject it, but fighting the will of God is futile, because it's going to happen.

Part of God's kingdom is here right now! Every time He uses someone to bless someone else, a dark corner in the world is illuminated, and a little piece of heaven shines through. His light and His truth are revealed through those who have accepted His Son as their Lord and Savior. They extend His kingdom by demonstrating the changes God wants to see in this world.

As the light continues to spread, it continues to reveal the wrongs in this fallen world. Humans will be able to see these wrongs, but they will be helplessly limited in correcting them. God will correct them by sending Jesus back to earth to fiercely avenge His enemies. The Second Coming of Jesus will usher in the full kingdom of God that is coming. But the actual day when Jesus returns will be hideously catastrophic, and the aftermath will be gruesome.

In the Old Testament, the Second Coming of Christ was known as the day of the LORD, the day when God would send the Messiah to make all things right for the Jewish people who believed in one almighty God. The ancient prophets frequently warned about the impending gloom and doom:

(1) "The Lord Almighty has a day in store for all the proud and lofty, for all that is exalted (and they will be humbled)" (Isaiah 2:12).

(2) "See, the day of the Lord is coming—a cruel day, with wrath and fierce anger—to make the land desolate and destroy the sinners within it" (Isaiah 13:9).
(3) "How awful that day will be! None will be like it!" (Jeremiah 30:7).
(4) "Let all who live in the land tremble, for the day of the Lord is coming. It is close at hand—a day of darkness and gloom, a day of clouds and blackness" (Joel 2:1,2).
(5) "The day of the Lord is great; it is dreadful. Who can endure it?" (Joel 2:11).
(6) "Woe to you who long for the day of the LORD ... That day will be darkness, not light" (Amos 5:18).
(7) "In the fire of His jealousy ... He will make a sudden end of all who live on the earth" (Zephaniah 1:18).

Wait a minute! The end of everyone living on earth? Then why are so many people currently saying, "Come, Lord Jesus ... come quickly"? Because they are the true Christians, and they won't be here when Jesus returns!

Jesus promised He was going to leave the earth to prepare a place for His followers in His Father's house. Then He will come back to take them with Him, so they can be with Him forever (John 14:3). Jesus is going to pull His church from the earth in a glorious event called the Rapture before He returns (1 Corinthians 15:51,52; 1 Thessalonians 4:16,17). The only people who will be left on earth are the ones who have continually rejected Jesus as their Lord and Savior, the ones who have regarded His commands as mere suggestions, the ones who have lived their lives to please themselves instead of pleasing God, and the ones who have continually rejected His messages.

Jesus will end their lives with the power of His Word: "Out of His mouth comes a sharp sword with which to strike the nations" (Revelation 19:15). All Jesus will do is speak, and heads are going to roll. Then the vultures will be summoned to clean up the carnage (Revelation 19:17, 18,21).

The world as we know it will not end when Jesus returns. The age of the church ... the age of the saints will end. The age of the King will begin.

# 47
## Millennium Era

After the world has been cleansed of unbelievers, Satan will be bound and sealed in a bottomless pit (the Abyss) for one thousand years (Revelation 20:1–3). Jesus will establish His kingdom and rule this millennium era as King of Kings, Lord of Lords, and Prince of Peace. He will demonstrate what happens when a righteous king rules over modern earth. All injustices will be corrected immediately. There will be no wars, uprisings, appeals, worries, fears, or pain. Wild animals will frolic but will not kill. The lion will lie down with the lamb. Good will triumph over evil. It's what the future for humankind is all about.

Nancy Leigh DeMoss captures these awesome promises in the following remarkable comparison.

**The Returning King**
(www.reviveourhearts.com/articles/returning-king)

He came the first time as an infant, born in time and space, small and weak. (Matt. 1:18–25; Luke 2:1–7)
He will return as the everlasting King, great in strength and glory. (Matt. 16:27a)

When He came the first time, His glory was shrouded, concealed from human view. (Phil. 2:5–8; 1 Cor. 2:6–8)
When He comes the second time, His glory will shine brightly. (Matt. 25:31)

His first coming was obscure, witnessed only by a few poor shepherds; few recognized who He was. (Luke 2:8–11)
At His second coming, every eye will see Him, and all will know who He is. (Rev. 1:7; Matt. 24:30a)

He came the first time as the Lamb of God. (Isa. 53:7; John 1:29; 1 Peter 1:19)
When He returns, it will be as the Lion of the tribe of Judah. (Gen. 49:9, 10; Rev. 5:5)

At His first coming, He was judged and condemned to die by sinful men. (Matt. 27:22, 23)
When He returns, it will be as the Judge, to execute justice and judgment on all who have refused to repent of their sins. (Isa. 16:5; Matt. 16:27b; 2 Thess. 1:7–9; Rev. 19:11b)

The first time He came as a Man of Sorrows. (Isa. 53:6; Luke 19:41; John 11:33)
When He returns, it will be as Almighty God. (Isa. 9:6; 49:26)

At His first advent, He rode into Jerusalem on a lowly donkey. (Luke 19:35,36)
When He returns, He will be riding on a great white horse. (Rev. 19:11–16)

When He came the first time, only a few bowed to pay Him homage. (Matt. 2:7–11; John 12:1–8)
When He returns, every knee will bow, and every tongue will confess that Jesus Christ is Lord. (Phil. 2:10,11)

The first time, He came to earth to die. (Matt. 10:28; John 3:17; 1 Tim. 1:15; 1 John 4:9, 10)
The second time, He will come to earth to reign. (Isa. 9:6, 7; Luke 1:30–33; Rev. 19:15b)

The first time, He came as a humble servant. (Phil. 2:5–8)
The second time, He will come as the Commander in Chief of the armies of heaven. (Rev. 19:14)

The first time, He washed the feet of His disciples. (John 13:3–5) When He returns, all His enemies will be under His feet. (1 Cor. 15:25)

The first time He came, He wore a crown of thorns. (Matt. 27:29; John 19:5)
When He returns, He will be crowned with many crowns, the King upon His throne. (Rev. 19:12)

He came the first time to make peace between God and man. (1 Tim. 2:5; 2 Cor. 5:18,19; Eph. 2:13,14)
When He returns, it will be to make war on those who have rebelled against Him. (Rev. 19:11; 2 Thess. 1:7–8)

He came the first time as our suffering Savior. (Ps. 22:1–18; 1 Peter 3:18)
He will return as our sovereign Lord. (1 Tim. 6:15, 16)

# 48
## The New Jerusalem

When the millennial era is over, a new heaven and earth will be created without any seas (Revelation 20:7; 21:1). A new holy city, called the New Jerusalem, will come down from heaven. Its dimensions seem to be that of a cube, a shape which was an ancient symbol for perfection. The most holy place in the Jewish temple was cubic in design.

The New Jerusalem will be about fourteen hundred miles in length, width, and height. Its gates will always remain open, because all things harmful to the city will have been destroyed. The walls will be about two hundred feet thick and made of clear jasper. The city will be made of clear gold, so it will be transparent, a symbol of purity and everlasting glory.

The beautiful city will not need sunlight or moonlight, because the glory of God will light it, and Jesus will hold the lamp (Revelation 21:23). God will live there with His people, His universal church, and His followers, whose names are written in the Lamb's Book of Life (Revelation 21:3, 27). They will be His people, and He will be their God, something He planned in the beginning of creation and reminded His people about frequently throughout the Bible. God will prevail.

# 49
## Is It Too Late?

Uh-oh! The Book of Life! What if we have been living largely for ourselves? What if our names have not been written in the Book of Life? Are we doomed? Is it too late to change our ways? Are we going to be left behind?

Not necessarily. As long as Christian saints are still in this world, we are still in the age of God's incredible mercies and graces, and it is not too late to sign up for His team.

Remarkably, God is still willing to forgive us for anything if we humble ourselves before Him by confessing our sins (known and unknown), expressing our genuine sorrow for what we have done wrong, asking for His forgiveness and assistance in turning from our ways, and starting the process of doing what is right in His eyes. Remember, God knows our hearts and our intentions. He just needs to hear them speak! If they are sincere, He will be delighted to help us and will write our names permanently in the Book of Life.

Is that fair to the people who have "walked the walk" for years? That is, people who have gone to church regularly, have believed in God, have tried to be good, have obeyed most laws, and have tried to be nice to others. Maybe not, but it's generous, and none of us should ever complain about God's many graces.

Need convincing? Read the parable about the workers in the vineyard (Matthew 20:1–16). It's the story of a landowner who hired men to work in his vineyard. He hired some of the workers in the morning, some at midday, and some in the late afternoon. At the end of the day, he surprised them by paying them all the same wages. The early workers were envious and irritated, typical human emotions.

The same parable is also the story of our Creator, who is very generous. God wants to save the souls of the latecomers as well as first-comers. "The last will be first and the first will be last" (Matthew 20:16). Are Christians resentful of people who live wayward lives and slip into heaven on their last breaths? No! True Christians appreciate the peace and empowerment of living in God's presence and know

200

the pecking order of salvation is not important. The invitation is the only thing that counts. They also know that life in this world is not fair, but life in the next world will be very fair, so they are actually looking for the wayward and the lost. They want others to know the joys of Christianity and to share its hopes and dreams by joining their family of sainthood.

Why should Christians care what happens to others? Because their job is to spread the kingdom of God on earth by letting Him work through them to bless others. True Christians are not human beings who are going through some spiritual experience. They are spiritual beings who are going through a difficult but temporary existence on earth, and they want to make it a better place for others as they pass through. They are sojourners on their way to their final destiny, and God is leading them. When they are called home, they hope to take others with them.

# 50
## Start the Process

How do people become better Christians? How do we start the process of doing what is right in God's eyes? By learning everything we can about God, His story, His choices, His people, His plan for humanity, and His specific plan for us.

### (1) Read the Bible!

Start with the *New International Version (NIV) Student Bible*. Many scholars believe this Bible has the closest English translation of the original Aramaic, which Jesus spoke, and Greek languages.

There are three study plans listed in the introduction. Use track 2; it will give you a tremendous overview of the entire Bible in six months if you read only fifteen minutes a day.

Once you have the big picture, you might enjoy focusing on ancient prophecies or some other areas of personal special interest. You can do this on your own or in structured Bible studies.

### (2) Go to Church!

Show your allegiance and thankfulness to God the Father, God the Son, and God the Holy Spirit by attending church regularly. But Be careful when choosing a church. Do a little research, and find a Bible-based, Christ-centered church. See if the congregation sings the *Gloria Patri* ("Glory be to the Father, and to the Son, and to the Holy Ghost"). See if the Apostle's Creed or Nicene Creed is recited. A congregation that believes in "God the Father Almighty, maker of heaven and earth, and in Jesus Christ, His only Son, our Lord..." is Bible-based, Christ-centered, and definitely heading in the right direction.

Churches have changed a lot in the past ten years! Some of the large, well-established churches across the country and throughout the world have buckled recently under public demand for "spiritual" leadership. Long-standing ministers are losing their jobs for not preaching "happy" sermons. More and more people are flocking to churches expecting to feel good about themselves and return home with the "warm fuzzies." They are into sensationalism. They want to hear about a benevolent God, who will assure them of a place in heaven if they do nice things for other people, contribute to charities, obey civic laws, attend church, and tithe. They don't want to hear about sin, punishment, Satan, hell, or the road less traveled. And they certainly don't want to hear about Jesus Christ! Be very wary of congregations that are into spirituality or religion. They are probably not into the Holy Spirit and are likely to jeopardize your dreams of spending eternity with the Lord.

**(3)  Learn to Live in Third Place!**
This sacrifice is called humility and means living behind God and others. You will have to acquire this asset, because humility goes directly against the natural, selfish, nature of humankind. Look for ways to help others, and keep your good deeds, charities, and sacrifices to yourself. Integrity can be measured by what you do when no one is looking. Know that God is always watching. He sees your efforts to please Him instead of pleasing society. His rewards will far surpass those of your friends and colleagues (Matthew 6:1–4; 6:19–21).

**(4)  Consider Being Baptized as an Adult!**
When Jesus came back to His disciples after his resurrection, He told them, "Go into all the world and preach the good news to all creation. Whoever believes and is baptized will be saved, but whoever does not believe will be condemned" (Mark 16:15, 16). After Jesus' ascension, Peter preached, "Repent and be baptized, every one of you, in the name of Jesus Christ for the forgiveness of your sins. And you will receive the gift of the Holy Spirit" (Acts 2:38).

Baptism is a very controversial subject among the various Christian denominations. Follow your heart and your calling. If you would like to know more about adult baptism, read *Muscle and a Shovel,* by Michael Shank. Michael is a rural preacher and teacher in southern Illinois, and the story is his account of his personal conversion.

**(5) Know that all Biblical Prophecy Is Centered on the Son of God and His Return!**
Beware of people who tell you ancient prophecy is a thing of the past and, therefore, not important or relevant to current events.

# 51
## Prophecy Is Significant

Prophecy has always been relevant to what's happening in the world, and it will be until the last one of the Second Coming has been fulfilled.

For over one hundred years, Noah told everyone to "Get on the boat!" He warned that God was going to make it rain and drown everyone who didn't come aboard. The people laughed, because they had never heard of rain. (The earth was watered by dew and underground springs in those days.) They didn't believe Noah, so they continued to live their lives as usual. And they all died. The eight people who survived the flood were all on the boat. Prophecy is relevant.

Lot told all the residents of Sodom and Gomorrah to clean up their immoral lives, because God was going to destroy their two cities with fire and brimstone—unless they started the long process of walking in His ways. The people laughed at Lot. Even his sons-in-law thought he was joking. All the residents carried on with their lives as before. And their cities were destroyed as prophesied. The only three survivors were Lot and his two daughters. Prophecy is relevant.

John the Baptist and Jesus preached repentance. They told people over and over that the kingdom of God is near. The kingdom is near. Prophecy is significant. Prophecy is the Word of God, and it's going to be very relevant five minutes after the Rapture, when the Christian saints are whisked off this earth into heaven to live with the Lord forever (1 Thessalonians 4:16, 17).

Most relevant of all, Jesus gave His disciples specific signs of what would be happening in the world shortly before the Rapture and before His return. See if these ring any bells.

(1) There will be wars and rumors of wars (Matthew 24:6). The Middle East? Iran? Russia? North Korea? China?

(2) There will be famines, earthquakes, and pestilence. Similar to birth pains, these will grow stronger and come closer together

(Matthew 24:7, 8). Famine in East Africa after the drought in 2011–2012? Famine in West Africa after the drought in 2012? Tsunamis? AIDS? MRSA? Ebola?

(3) False prophets will appear and deceive many people (Matthew 24:11). Charles Manson? Jim Jones? David Koresh?

(4) Christians will be persecuted for their faith in Jesus Christ (Matthew 24:9). Atheists and radical Islamists versus Christians?

Look around. All these things are happening right now, and much to our dismay, the industrialized nations of the world are becoming increasingly immersed in trends of terrorism, violent crimes, substance abuse, sexual immorality, fraud, identity theft, corrupt leadership, economic chaos, and covetousness of everybody and everything. Reverence for God and respect for others have been replaced by self-reverence and a love for power, money, popularity, and sensationalism.

How much longer do you think God is going to restrain His wrath against arrogant, stiff-necked humankind? Based on current world events and the dire straits of Israel right now, probably not much longer. No one, including Jesus, knows when God will send His Son back to earth (Matthew 24:36), and we are not to hazard guesses. But great future events always cast long shadows, and the shadows continue to lengthen today, especially behind Israel.

God has warned us that He will bless those who bless Israel and curse those who curse it (Genesis 12:3). Israel is His timepiece, and the nations that support it today are clearly separated from those that oppose it. Israel is surrounded by countries with nuclear weapons and tenacious determination to wipe it off the face of our earth. God is not going to let His chosen people be annihilated, so it is reasonable to assume that millions of people might leave this earth suddenly, any day now, before Jesus returns to avenge His enemies.

God loves us all unconditionally, which far surpasses our limited human understanding. He does not expect us to understand His transcending love, but He does expect us to accept it and know that

He doesn't want anyone to be left behind. He expects us to change our lives if they are going on and on as usual. He expects us to "get on the boat" and get on it now. He expects us to ask Him for help to walk away from what's wrong and toward what's right, while we still have a choice.

Ancient prophecy is what helps us make those still available good choices! Our knowledge of the future gives us a better perspective of the present and keeps us from being alarmed at what's happening now or frightened of things that are going to happen. Prophecy assures Christians that we won't be here on earth when Christ returns, so we are not looking for God's vengeance to descend on us. We are looking for our Lord and Savior to call us home with Him before He descends on those left behind. "For God did not appoint us to suffer wrath, but to receive salvation through our Lord Jesus Christ" (1 Thessalonians 5:9).

Prophecy allows Christians to be thermostats instead of thermometers, as the fallen world appears to get away with irreverence for God and very little respect or compassion for others. Knowing that God has a very special plan for His own, we can set ourselves to remain composed and positive instead of wringing our hands and hanging our heads. Stay positive! Things might seem dark and backward right now, but don't focus on what's seen. Focus on the unseen, for what is seen is temporary, but what is unseen is eternal (2 Corinthians 4:18). Focus on God's promises. Wait for the Lord. Know that good will prevail over evil in the long run (Psalm 37). Prophecy allows us to encourage others to keep standing up for God's principles and commandments, because we know all the future prizes behind the closed doors!

No one is going to lead a messed-up life by choosing to walk in God's ways. But plenty of people will lead messed-up lives for choosing to walk in their own ways, just because they foolishly regard God's commandments as infringements on their inalienable right of freedom. God's commandments are not infringements! They were not given to take the pizazz out of our lives. They were given to keep us in the realm of His many, many blessings. His laws, along with His promises to protect those who obey them, actually make our lives very secure.

The people who kick God out of their homes, schools, courthouses, government and military so they can be free to live by their own set of rules will eventually spiral downhill. As they get swept up in today's world of self-absorption and consistently choose what is popular, what *feels* good, or what *seems* right, they will eventually realize the hokey pokey is not what this world is all about. They are the ones who will become haunted by insecurities, meaninglessness, and despair.

Stand away from them. "Do not conform any longer to the pattern of this world" (Romans 12:2). Stand with the children of the Light, who know the Lord (1 Thessalonians: 5:5) and are going toward that Light. Stand up for good morals, sound principles, true beliefs, and lasting values. Stand up for God! If the leaders of our world stood up for the principles of God, we wouldn't be in the mess we are in today.

Don't worry about the state of the world. It is in God's hands. If it is crumbling, there is a reason. If it is falling down, look up, because your redemption is drawing near (Luke 21:28). What is redemption? It is a price already paid to secure the release of something or someone. Our release from the fallen world? Absolutely! Therefore, look up and see the bright side of things. Realize that Jesus paid for all our wrongs when He died on the cross for us. He bought us, but He left us in a fallen world. He has not redeemed us yet. He is still working through us to make the world a better place for the downtrodden. He rewards those who learn His will and walk in His ways. And, He is coming back to take us home with Him. Praise God. Stand up and cheer!

# Conclusion
## We Have Forgotten God's Love

Jesus' last words to His eleven apostles before His ascension were, "Surely I am with you always to the very end of the age" (Matthew 28:20). What age? This age, the age of the church, the age of the Holy Spirit

When Jesus calls His church—His followers—out of this world, He will whisk them to heaven with Him "in a twinkling of an eye" (1 Corinthians 15:52; 1 Thessalonians 4:16,17). When He returns one day, He will bring His followers with Him as enthusiastic spectators (Revelation 19:14).

His promise is still there for all of us who will listen. Having Jesus in our lives empowers us to rise above our circumstances and make our lives meaningful. But it seems we have forgotten His promise.

Won't you join His forces? He is not looking for indentured servitude on earth. He is looking for volunteers. He has already conquered the world and done all the work. He is looking for recruiters. He is looking for people to extend His kingdom by reflecting His warm light, His "Sonshine". He is looking for little flashlights who can lead the way to Him. He is looking for little hinges who can help others open His awesome door. Please lend Him your hand.

God bless you!

Printed in the United States
By Bookmasters